IEP Guide
for
All

IEP Guide
for
All

**What Parents and Teachers Need to Know
About Individualized Education Programs**

Jennifer Laviano and Julie Swanson

Skyhorse Publishing

Skyhorse Publishing books may be purchased in bulk at special discounts for sales
promotion, corporate gifts, fund-raising, or educational purposes. Special editions can
also be created to specifications. For details, contact the Special Sales Department,
Skyhorse Publishing, 307 West 36th Street, 11th Floor, New York, NY 10018 or
info@skyhorsepublishing.com.

Skyhorse® and Skyhorse Publishing® are registered trademarks of Skyhorse
Publishing, Inc.®, a Delaware corporation.

Visit our website at www.skyhorsepublishing.com.

Please follow our publisher Tony Lyons on Instagram @tonylyonsisuncertain.

10 9 8 7 6 5 4 3 2 1

Library of Congress Cataloging-in-Publication Data is available on file.

Print ISBN: 978-1-64821-023-5
eBook ISBN: 978-1-64821-066-2

Cover design by Matt Veligdan
Cover photo by Iakov Filimonov

Printed in the United States of America

For *our* first advocates . . . our moms

"There's nobody in line behind you to advocate for your child."
—Janet Swanson

"You're only ever as happy as your unhappiest child."
—Donna Laviano

CONTENTS

FOREWORD

by Attorney Melissa Gagne

This is the book I needed as a young parent, navigating the world of special education with a son who was newly diagnosed with severe autism. This is the book I needed as a new school principal, responsible for the appropriate special education programming for the students in my building. And this is the book I now look forward to recommending to IEP teams, as a special education attorney, to inspire both school districts and families to find the best solutions for the children in their care.

As a law partner to one of the authors, and as someone deeply familiar with both the legal intricacies and the personal challenges faced by families navigating the special education system, I am honored to introduce this remarkable book. Coauthored by Jennifer Laviano, a dynamic and experienced special education attorney, and Julie Swanson, an accomplished special education parent and advocate, it represents a beacon of hope and empowerment for parents, educators, and advocates alike as they endeavor to create meaningful and effective **Individualized Education Programs (IEPs)** for children with disabilities.

Throughout my career, I have witnessed the transformative power of a well-crafted IEP. For parents, it can be the difference between frustration and empowerment, between uncertainty and clarity. Reflecting on my own journey, I am reminded of the myriad of emotions that accompany the discovery of a child's disability. There is the initial shock, grief, the waves of uncertainty, and the overwhelming desire to do everything in your power to ensure your child's well-being and future success. As a parent, these feelings are amplified by the weight of responsibility and the fear of the unknown. It's a journey filled with highs and lows, victories and setbacks, but above all, it's a journey fueled by love, determination, and relentless advocacy.

In my former role within schools, I witnessed firsthand the challenges faced by educators tasked with meeting the diverse needs of their students. Balancing academic rigor with individualized support is no small feat, particularly when faced with limited resources and competing demands. Yet, I also witnessed the profound impact that a collaborative approach between parents, educators, and advocates can have on the success and well-being of children with disabilities.

Now, as a special education attorney, I am humbled by the opportunity to pay forward the invaluable support and guidance that I received. This book represents more than just a manual for navigating the legal complexities of special education; it is a testament to the enduring bonds of community, empathy, and advocacy.

What sets this book apart is its unique blend of legal expertise and practical guidance. By marrying the insights of a seasoned attorney with the firsthand experience of a dedicated advocate, Jennifer and Julie have created a comprehensive roadmap for navigating the complexities of the IEP process. From understanding the legal framework to developing meaningful goals and accommodations, this book equips readers with the tools and knowledge they need to advocate effectively for their children and students.

To the parents who may be feeling overwhelmed or uncertain: please know that you are not alone. This book is a testament to the power of knowledge, advocacy, and community in ensuring that every child receives the support they need to succeed. And to the educators who tirelessly champion the needs of their students: I urge you to embrace the principles of collaboration and partnership outlined in these pages. By working together with parents and families, you can create IEPs that truly reflect the individual needs and aspirations of each child. May this book serve as a guiding light on your journey towards creating Individualized Education Programs that unlock the full potential of every child.

PREFACE

"Education is not the filling of a pail, but the lighting of a fire."
—William Butler Yeats

In our many years of representing thousands of families at the IEP Team Meeting table, we have found that one of the biggest obstacles to students getting what they need is the lack of understanding about the IEP process itself, and what the law requires it to include. This is a challenge for parents and educators alike! Unfortunately, we believe school districts could do a better job at providing both groups the information and training they need to be truly prepared to develop IEPs that provide meaningful educational benefit. We know that many efforts are made by administrations to provide professional development, but we feel strongly this is an area that in many places needs improvement.

The mere fact that you are reading this book means you are ahead of many parents and educators and well on your way to improving the outcomes for children with disabilities! Just knowing the eight legally required elements of an IEP mandated by federal law is a huge start toward complying with the IDEA (Individuals with Disabilities Education Act) and ensuring that the student or students you are serving receive meaningful education plan.

If you are an educator, we want to truly thank you for wading through the legalese and sometimes confusing portions of the statutory language of the IDEA. We know that you did not necessarily become an educator because you wanted to become an expert in reading legislation! The fact that you care enough to take the time to become more informed on this topic means the world to us as advocates for children with disabilities, and more importantly, it can forever alter your students' future for the better.

If you are a parent or otherwise connected to a student with a disability, we know that the Annual IEP Meeting can be the meeting you most dislike attending every year, not to mention the other IEP meetings you may have throughout the school year! We get it, but we hope that by understanding what that IEP must include, you will become empowered to change that. Your participation is vital to the process, and while it can be daunting to read the legal requirements and make sense of it, we know for certain that the children whose parents are informed about their rights in this process learn more with greater results.

The "paperwork" can seem like it focuses on minutiae, instead of the big picture of how the student is doing and whether they are being educated. However, in reviewing the required elements of the IEP, we hope you realize why Congress created the legally mandated elements of the document. If each and every one of those items is discussed, agreed upon, and properly recorded in the IEP, the program itself will be appropriate.

Far too often, parents and educators feel "at odds" with one another when they are developing the IEP. So, we leave you with the following: all students will be better served if the adults in their lives stay singularly focused on creating IEPs which comply with the law and are created in a way that honors their entitlement to a Free and Appropriate Public Education.

INTRODUCTION

Why THIS book? There are hundreds if not thousands of resources online, and many books regarding IEPs. Why should you devote your very precious time to reading this one?

That's a fair question. Here is our answer: because it will actually help you improve the IEP for your student or child.

When we wrote our first book, *Your Special Education Rights: What Your School District Isn't Telling You,* we were passionate about bringing basic information about the IDEA to parents. As professionals who saw how different the quality of education is for students whose parents understand their rights and how to navigate the incredibly confusing and bureaucratic special education system, we wanted to "boil it down" to the basics that families need to know in order to advocate for their child. We have been so thrilled with the feedback we have gotten from our readers, who have told us time and time again that they wish they had our book at the beginning of their child's special education journey. What we hear over and over is appreciation for making the information short, simple, and meaningful.

What we were perhaps not expecting was how many educators reached out to us about the book as well. While we devoted an entire chapter in the first book to the rights and concerns of educators ("Teachers Need to Eat, Too"), our primary audience was parents. But we have learned through incredible feedback from teachers all over the country who have read our book, listened to our podcasts, and worked with the children we represent that educators need our direct, honest, "gloves off" approach now more than ever before. *This* book is for everyone!

The *IEP Guide for All* is designed to break down the statutorily prescribed elements of an IEP in a user-friendly way. We tell you what the law literally states and then interpret that legalese into easy-to-understand terms. Most importantly, we give parents and educators the "must-know" takeaway on that aspect of the IEP. In essence, we distill the legal into the practical for you, so that you can leave your IEP Meetings knowing that you understand what that IEP must include, and that you have actually included it.

> Leaving aside what the law requires of school districts, advocating for the rights of individuals with disabilities is an inherent moral imperative of any society. Indeed, it is an inherent moral imperative of any human.

It is our greatest hope that after reading this book, and continuing to use it over time, you will be empowered to develop IEPs that do what the law requires, and our system and *consciences* dictate: to create educational programs that are individualized and designed to ensure that students with disabilities receive an appropriately meaningful public education.

HOW TO READ THIS BOOK

In our first book, *Your Special Education Rights: What Your School District Isn't Telling You*, we created a comprehensive handbook for understanding the special education laws and almost all things related to advocating for children with disabilities. We highly encourage you to read it, as it covers a more global view of the rights of students with special needs and the ins and outs of how public schools work. It is a great companion to this book. The *IEP Guide for All* is primarily focused on the IEP document itself and is designed to be a tool for IEP Team Members to use in the development of IEPs for students with disabilities. As such, it includes a breakdown of each of the eight components outlined by the IDEA that *must* be incorporated into the written IEP document.

Don't forget to check your own local and state policies and laws to see if there are different or additional requirements for an IEP beyond what the federal law requires.

PART ONE
SOME BACKGROUND

NOTE TO PARENTS

Is your child's Annual IEP Review the worst day of your year? Would you rather have a root canal than attend this meeting? Do IEP Meetings in general leave you feeling alone, scared, intimidated, and like you have possibly let your child down because you didn't understand the terminology, your rights, and the process? Are you having panic attacks and feel like you need to take medication to get through these meetings? Do you wish it *didn't have to be this hard?*

We hear you, and we have answers for you.

If we can point to any one factor that will transform the outcome for your child and the effectiveness of your advocacy for them, it is knowing your rights and how to assert them. There is no place where that is more important than the IEP Table. The IEP document is

> Knowledge is power. The more you know about what your child's IEP Team is required to do, and your right to participate in every aspect of the development of that IEP, the less you will fear those IEP Meetings!

the legal contract that exists between you and your child's school district as to what they will be providing. Any disagreement about what a student requires, whether a minor quibble over a related service or a major legal dispute, starts with an analysis of the IEP document. If the question is whether your child is receiving the services you agreed upon, the first place to look is the IEP. If the question is whether the IEP itself is designed to offer your child a Free and Appropriate Public Education (FAPE), the first place to look is the IEP. If the question is whether your school has complied with their procedural obligations, the first place to look is . . . you guessed it, the IEP.

We cannot overstate how essential it is that you understand what an IEP must include and how you go about ensuring that your child's IEP incorporates all federally mandated elements.

Just like anything else important in life, meaningful participation in the development of an IEP requires preparation. The most important step of preparation for parents is understanding what the school district is required to do, and what they MUST include in an IEP for it to pass legal muster.

Congress did not impose the legal obligation of the required IEP elements and attach the funding associated with IDEA compliance without reason. Their rationale going back to the 1970s when the statute was enacted was to ensure that if the plan (as documented in the IEP) included all the required elements, the school team would be held accountable to make sure the plan was followed. Presumably, this would result in the student actually learning and receiving an appropriate education.

Look, here is the cold, hard reality: You have been given the task of raising a child who has disabilities. You are probably already an expert on things you never dreamed you'd need to

> We always urge parents to collaborate with the school team to foster a good relationship with them. This isn't always an easy task when you may need to challenge the process or the team. Effectively advocating for your child requires that you strike a balance between robust advocacy and maintaining a respectful relationship.

know about your child's diagnosis or diagnoses. And now we're telling you to become an expert on the laws around special education too? Yes, unfortunately, we are.

Whether you like it or not, you have to know at least as much as the team does, if not more. The good news is you don't need to be a lawyer to understand the basics, and this book is going to give you what you must know to be an effective member of your child's IEP team.

So, buckle up and let's get started!

NOTE TO EDUCATORS

So, you work for a school district. Perhaps you are a special educator or regular education teacher. Or maybe you are a paraprofessional or student aide. You might be a related service provider like
a speech and language pathologist, occupational therapist, physical therapist, counselor, or school psychologist. You might also be
someone who works at a school and has no direct teaching role
with students. Are you a school nurse or librarian?

Maybe you work at a school, and you wonder whether you can
refer a child to be evaluated for special education eligibility.

All of you touch the lives of students and make significant
contributions to their development academically, socially, emo-
tionally, or behaviorally as students who are learning vital skills
for life.

Does the IEP process, much less the writing of an IEP, scare
the heck out of you? Does it seem like every different school
you have worked in has a totally different approach to the writing of IEPs, and you just want to know what the IEP *must*
include?

Or maybe you are feeling intimidated by this process for other reasons. Perhaps you have realized that your school does not encourage you to be forthcoming about what students need when you attend IEP meetings. Worse, you might even have been directed by

In extreme circumstances, Section 504 of the Rehabilitation Act as well as many Collective Bargaining Agreements between teachers' unions and school districts protect educators from being unlawfully retaliated against for advocating for the rights of individuals with disabilities.

your administration on what to say and what not to say at an IEP meeting. Do you wish you could voice your true opinion about what your student needs?

We hear you and we have answers.

Perhaps it's been many years since you received any instruction or training on the special rights of children with disabilities. Or maybe you just started teaching. Whether you are a new educator or a seasoned professional, the fact is that you bring value to your role as an educator and, as such, should have command over the law that protects your students and your position on the IEP (Individualized Education Program) team.

Further, in getting down to the nitty gritty of the legislative purposes of several portions of the IEP, you will start to understand why you are required to fill out some of the forms and paperwork that seem to never end. It is our hope this will make it less frustrating to perform this part of your job.

So, roll up your sleeves and get ready to empower yourself as a valued and informed member of your students' IEP team.

WHAT IS AN IEP AND WHERE DOES IT COME FROM?

The *IEP Guide for All* is a manual for parents, educators, and any individual who needs to know about IEPs in their personal or professional capacity. Most of you have a child or a student you are working with who requires an IEP and have attended many IEP meetings yourself. But some of you may be brand-spanking-new to this process, so let's break it down to the basics. It's not rocket science, but it can feel that way, so let's demystify IEPs.

WHAT IS AN IEP?

An IEP is an Individualized Education Program. It is a written document that operates like a contract between a parent of a child with a disability and that child's school district. It outlines what services, supports, and accommodations the student will receive. Basically, it summarizes, in detail, the student's special education plan.

A "Child with a Disability" who qualifies for an IEP is a child "with intellectual disabilities, hearing impairments (including deafness), speech or language impairments, visual impairments (including blindness), serious emotional disturbance (referred to in this title as 'emotional disturbance'), ortho-

> Your state may have additional or somewhat different eligibility classifications. However, the IEP Team does not have to agree on a "label" prior to providing special education and related services to the student. 20 USC 1412(a)(3)(B)

pedic impairments, autism, traumatic brain injury, other health impairments, or specific learning disabilities . . . who by reason thereof needs special education and related services."[1]

The law defines an IEP as "a written statement for each child with a disability that is developed, reviewed, and revised . . ." in accordance with the requirements outlined by the IDEA's detailed description of what needs to be included in an IEP for it to be legally sufficient. So, the IEP comes from the IDEA.

WHAT IS THE IDEA?

The IDEA is the Individuals with Disabilities Education Act. It is the federal law which requires public schools in every state and US territory to identify, evaluate, and program for students who meet the eligibility criteria of being a "child with a disability" who requires specialized instruction in school. The IDEA has been in effect since it was enacted by Congress in 1975.[2] All public school districts in the United States are required to follow the federal law, since all of them have chosen to receive the federal funding attached to the Act. So yes, the IDEA exists in your school district, too, and while each state is permitted by law to offer additional support and services above and beyond the IDEA, they cannot offer fewer. Think of the federal law as the floor of entitlement, not the ceiling, in your own jurisdiction. We mention this

---

1 20 USC 1401

2 Originally titled the Education for All Handicapped Children Act.

because we have heard from far too many parents who attend our presentations, "I was told they don't have to do that here." Yes, they do. Every single state and territory must follow the IDEA!

A common misconception is that public magnet and charter schools do not have to follow the IDEA. Charter and magnet schools are required to follow the IDEA and Section 504 as publicly funded entities.

A relatively easy way to conceptualize the IDEA is that it has two intersecting obligations on local school districts and state educational agencies: the obligation to follow the procedures and the obligation to offer a student with a disability a Free and Appropriate Educational Program (FAPE). Think of the procedures as the "rules" of the IDEA. These include things like the obligation to hold an IEP meeting at least annually; the obligation to re-evaluate a child in all suspected areas of disability at least every three years; the obligation to invite parents to the IEP meeting and work to ensure their participation; the obligation to have a regular education teacher at the IEP meeting if the student will be participating in the general education curriculum; etc.

In addition to the rules and procedures, each school year a school district must offer to each IDEA-eligible child a Free and Appropriate Public Education (FAPE). Yes, in order for the FAPE requirement to be met, the school has to have complied with the procedures, but the ultimate question is whether the IEP is designed to result in a meaningful education for the child. Indeed, a violation of the procedures is only legally relevant if that violation results in a deprivation of educational benefit for the student. More simply put, it's important to follow the procedures *and* to provide a free and appropriate education. But be aware, sometimes when the procedures are not followed, the procedural violations do *not* result in an inappropriate program, and sometimes they *do*.

WHAT IS AN IEP NOT?

(It is not a 504 Plan)

The IDEA is a completely separate statute from Section 504 of the Rehabilitation Act. Some students who have disabilities require a 504 Plan, rather than an IEP. There are many similarities between these two laws, but the core difference is that a child who requires an IEP needs "specialized instruction" in addition to accommodations, whereas Section 504 is primarily an accommodations act. An easy example is a student who has a peanut allergy. They may need certain accommodations in the cafeteria or classroom, but they don't need to be *taught* differently. A harder example are students who have ADHD, mental health challenges, or other disabilities which sometimes rise to the level of requiring specialized instruction, and sometimes do not. The IEP Team should review whether a student is eligible under the IDEA and qualifies for an IEP after conducting comprehensive testing in all suspected areas of disability. 20 USC 1414

> Whether a student is a "child with a disability" under the IDEA or qualifies under Section 504 can only be determined after the school team has evaluated the student in all suspected areas of disability.

This book is largely devoted to describing the legally required elements of an IEP. It is a guide to assist IEP Team Members (including parents) in making sure they are writing the document in a way that includes all the elements Congress has said

> One of the best indicators that an IEP will serve the child well is that ALL team members have fully engaged in an open dialogue about what the student needs.

an IEP must have to be procedurally sufficient. HOWEVER, just because an IEP includes all the federally required elements does not necessarily mean the IEP is appropriate. An IEP document can look gorgeous, can have every single part the law dictates it must have on paper, but still not be one that offers the student in question an appropriate education. We want you to know that pretty paperwork doesn't mean the program is resulting in a quality education for that child!

That said, you will be far more likely to have an IEP that is offering a child a substantively appropriate education if you are sure that it includes all eight of the federally required elements (covered in this book in Part 2), and as importantly, that the IEP Team, *including the parents,* discusses each and every one of them.

> Each public agency must ensure that a continuum of alternative placements is available to meet the needs of children with disabilities for special education and related services. 34 CFR 300.115

Finally, we stress this point here and as often as we can: NEVER forget the "I" in IEP. Individualization is the core to appropriate programming. Too frequently IEP teams offer children what they have, rather than what a particular child requires based on their unique needs.

Educators and related professionals, we caution you to avoid "cookie cutter" IEPs that look almost identical for every child with that disability in your school. Parents, we caution you to not simply accept the IEP, or parts of it, if you don't agree. Provide your input and have discussions to work out your different thoughts before an IEP becomes finalized. If you are given a choice between two or three options, none of which meet your child's unique needs, make it clear you don't believe your child has been offered an IEP that is individualized.

THE DREADED IEP PAPERWORK

"The devil is in the details."
—Unknown

As cliche as the saying "the devil is in the details" is, we could not think of a better phrase to capture the dreaded IEP paperwork. This idiom generally alludes to a "loophole" or mysterious element hidden in the fine print. It indicates that though something may seem basic, if you don't pay attention to exactly how it is written, problems can arise later.

WHAT PARENTS NEED TO KNOW

Here are the common refrains we hear from parents about the IEP and its paperwork:

"I don't have time to read it."

"I don't understand it."

"It overwhelms me."

"I just trust what the school team puts in the IEP. They are the educators."

Can you relate to any of these sentiments? Are you guilty of any of these sentiments? If so, imagine us sitting you down right now and telling you this is where this approach to the IEP paperwork ends for you! No, we mean it. And don't worry, we're going to tell you what you can do to change your habits.

First, you should know that we are passionate about parents understanding their rights under the IDEA. In fact, we devoted a video-based website to teaching parents the basics of the IDEA and IEP process called YourSpecialEducationRights.com. We also devoted our first book to helping parents understand how the special education process works.

We feel strongly that parents must understand the basics. You don't have to go crazy, but we want you to know enough to know when something's not right. This begins with the IEP paperwork.

So how can we help you understand the paperwork?

You should know that one of the related services[3] under the IDEA is Parent Counseling and Training. We aren't fond of the term "parent training" because it implies you might not know how to parent your child. Unfortunately, there are some terms in IDEA that we wish they had asked us about first because they aren't the best choice of words. But getting over that, parent counseling and training means: "assisting parents in understanding the special needs of their child; providing parents with information about child development; and helping parents to acquire the necessary skills that will allow them to support the implementation of their child's IEP."[4]

Bingo, there it is. Parent counseling allows you to "support the implementation of your child's IEP." We simply love this "related service" because it allows parents to ask the school team to provide

---

3 Sec. 300.34 Related services means transportation and such developmental, corrective, and other supportive services as are required to assist a child with a disability to benefit from special education, and includes speech-language pathology and audiology services, interpreting services, psychological services, physical and occupational therapy, recreation, including therapeutic recreation, early identification and assessment of disabilities in children, counseling services, including rehabilitation counseling, orientation and mobility services, and medical services for diagnostic or evaluation purposes. Related services also include school health services and school nurse services, social work services in schools, and parent counseling and training.

4 34 CFR 300.34 (c)(8)

you with the support around this complicated and overwhelming process. It is sadly underutilized in our experience.

To understand the paperwork, which you need to do in order to understand how the IEP is implemented, we suggest requesting that your school district instruct you on your state's IEP paperwork. Bring this book with you and show them how this book details the eight federally mandated areas of the IEP. Ask the person who has been assigned to review the IEP with you to show you where all eight areas are on the paperwork and how the document flows.

WHAT EDUCATORS AND RELATED PROFESSIONALS NEED TO KNOW

We know it's not easy being an educator and keeping up with the paperwork. We respect you immensely and understand how much work goes into the documents and forms that go with the Herculean task of teaching.

We don't want to tell you how to do your job because we know you most likely got into this field because you love kids and teaching them. But here are some things we hear frequently from teachers and related educational professionals about the IEP process:

"I feel like I spend more time filling out paperwork than I do teaching."

"The forms don't make any sense."

"This is busywork."

"Most of the stuff in the IEPs are just good educational strategies anyway."

"I would do these things for any child I work with."

We do understand that the IEP paperwork can frequently seem like just another focus on minutiae forced upon you by state and federal legislators. Your time spent actually teaching the students you work with is probably the time you most treasure in your job. So, we can understand why sitting for hours in IEP meetings, not to mention the great amount of planning and preparation that goes into your recommendations, is probably cumbersome.

However, following the procedures and ensuring that every child's IEP has what the law requires is essential.

Please remember that attached to the IEP document is a mother, a father, a family, a caretaker or loved one who has nothing in life more worth advocating for than their child.

And regardless of the level of commitment of the parents or family, *attached to every IEP is a child who needs your help.*

You are reading this book because you want to know more about how to work with the children in your school. That is commendable and greatly appreciated by us! We hope that your school district fully supports you in providing you ongoing training on the IEP process so that you can be sure you are up to date on what is expected of you.

If you use this manual as a starting point for your role as an IEP Team Member, you will hopefully begin to understand that Congress didn't create these obligations to torture educators, but rather to ensure that students with disabilities receive the Free and Appropriate Public Education to which they are entitled.

WHAT *ALL* IEP TEAM MEMBERS SHOULD KNOW

Once you've gotten your training, we suggest you read every new IEP you receive. Don't worry, we're going to make it as simple as possible. Get yourself a few different color highlighters, or pull out your computer or tablet, whatever works for you to stay organized. Sit yourself down with a cup of coffee or tea or whatever prepares you to deal with this task. We promise it will get easier as you practice it more frequently.

Every state's paperwork is different, so we can't instruct you on this process in a cookie-cutter fashion. But since all states must include these eight areas, we're starting with that.

Since the "present levels"[5] are the foundation of the IEP and from which all IEP goals flow, take your favorite color highlighter or grab your iPad, and highlight each area.

---

5 Chapter 1 in this book.

Each state may use different language for the areas, but categories should include domains like:

- o Academic skills
- o Daily living or self-help skills
- o Communication skills
- o Behavior
- o Social
- o Emotional
- o Health
- o Sensory skills—hearing, seeing
- o Mobility—getting around in school and the community

Perhaps in a different color, highlight the language that captures the lagging skills included in the written statements. Now you have each area highlighted and the skills that have been prioritized for targeting in the IEP. These are the weaknesses that have an adverse impact on your child participating and making progress in that area.

If you do nothing more than this, you are miles ahead of the game in understanding the dreaded IEP paperwork and how the IEP flows.

Now, go through each of the other required elements, and find where they exist on the IEP forms in your school district. Remember, your state's paperwork may not use the same wording for each of the eight federally mandated areas. In your training, identify each section that corresponds with these areas.

We promise you that your eyes will be dramatically opened when you've invested some time in breaking the IEP down into these areas. Remember, it's a whole new you—a you who can confidently say you know where all of the eight required elements of an IEP are for this child. You're going to be enlightened and empowered.

PROCEDURAL SAFEGUARDS:
A BASIC UNDERSTANDING

This is not a fully encompassing book on special education, or special education law, but rather a very specific manual for understanding the IEP—the document and all the elements that go into it. However, we think it's important for parents and educators to have a handle on the basic procedural safeguards that drive the special education process, so we included a quick and easy reference to the basics.

In *Your Special Education Rights,* we used Jerry Seinfeld's quote "We're all playing the game, but the lawyers read the top of the box" to illustrate the concept of the Procedural Safeguards in IDEA. The easiest way to look at them is that they are the rules, the legally required steps that go into the development of an IEP.

If your child has an IEP, you are familiar with the procedural safeguard documentation that the school mails you, physically gives you at an IEP meeting, or makes you aware of in a digital form. In our experience, this document is rarely examined by parents. It is rarely examined even by our clients who are lawyers!

The response we hear from parents when we ask them if they are aware of their procedural safeguards is, "Oh yeah, I got that, but I've never looked at it," or "It was way too confusing, so I didn't read it."

If you are an educator or related professional, you are likely familiar with the concept of the procedural safeguards, but have you read them? Have you had any training or professional development on what they mean and how you can be sure you are following them? As an educator, parents may well ask you to explain the procedural requirements to them, and we are sure that you want to feel confident in answering them.

We understand how overwhelming they are, but they are the rules of the road of special education from a process perspective, and we want you to understand them on at least a basic level. They exist to protect the rights of children with disabilities and their parents, so they are very important. The hope and expectation is that, if the procedures are followed properly, the resulting IEP will be substantively appropriate. In other words, the document won't just look pretty "on paper," it will actually result in a plan that will educate the student.

So, what are the procedural safeguards?

Procedural safeguards protect the rights of children with disabilities and their parents. These safeguards include:

- An opportunity for parents to examine their child's records.[6]
- The right to participate in meetings with their child's school relating to the identification eligibility and eligibility category, evaluation, and educational placement proposed, and related to whether the student was provided a Free and Appropriate Public Education (FAPE).
- The right to Independent Educational Evaluation of their child.

---

6 This is a separate obligation from the parents' right to a copy of their child's educational records under a different federal law, FERPA.

- Protection of the rights of children whose parents cannot be located, including homeless children and wards of the state.

> Independent Educational Evaluations (IEEs) is a parent's "second opinion" on their child's needs obtained from an evaluator who is not employed by the district, and at public expense. The obligations on district responses to IEE requests is complex and could be an entire book itself.

- Written Prior Notice to the parents whenever the school proposes to initiate or change, or refuses to initiate or change, the identification, evaluation, or educational placement of their child,[7] which written notice must be in the native language of the parents when feasible.
- An opportunity for Mediation and the procedures governing this process.
- An opportunity to file a Due Process Complaint[8] and the procedures governing this process.
- The requirement that parents are given a copy of their Procedural Safeguards at least annually.
- The requirement that a Resolution Session be offered once an Impartial Due Process Hearing is requested.
- The right to bring counsel and the parents' entitlement to ask for reasonable attorneys' fees if they prevail in an Impartial Due Process Hearing.
- The procedure for appealing Hearing decisions.
- The right to maintain the student in the current educational placement if there is a disagreement on a change in placement, including those in the context of disciplinary referrals such as expulsion.
- The obligation of the district to hold a "Manifestation Determination" with the IEP Team to ascertain whether

---

7 Many refer to this as Prior Written Notice (PWN).

8 As with many of the terms under the IDEA, this is one where many States and districts use their own language: Due Process Hearing; Impartial Hearing; Impartial Due Process Hearing, etc.

This is the portion of the procedural safeguards referred to as "stay put" and/or "pendency." It is the right of a parent to appeal a decision made by an IEP Team through a Due Process Hearing, during which time the student's placement cannot be lawfully changed by the district, with some exceptions (namely in the area of illegal substances/drugs, weapons, and causing bodily injury). Stay put does not simply apply to disciplinary referrals, however. It is a right for the parents to assert whenever the district proposes a change in the child's placement, including a recommendation to graduate from high school if the parent and student disagree with the graduation. In many jurisdictions, parents must act very quickly to assert this right.

any alleged misconduct was "caused by, or had a direct and substantial relationship to, the child's disability, OR if "the conduct in question was the direct result of the local educational agency's failure to implement the IEP" before a student's placement may be changed, and the exceptions to that process.

- Protections for students who are suspected of having a disability but have not yet been determined eligible for an IEP in the context of disciplinary removals.
- The process for transferring the rights of a child from the parents to the student upon the student reaching the age of majority.

As you can see, the procedural safeguards are lengthy, highly complex, and detailed. There are many experienced lawyers who don't always agree on what they mean, and we aren't suggesting that you become a scholar on this subject. However, the procedures are designed to ensure that the IEP itself will involve the key stakeholders in a student's education, whose meaningful participation in the development of the IEP will result in an appropriate program.

PART TWO
REQUIRED ELEMENTS
OF AN IEP

CHAPTER 1

PRESENT LEVELS OF ACADEMIC ACHIEVEMENT AND FUNCTIONAL PERFORMANCE

"The loftier the building, the deeper must the foundation be laid."
—Thomas A. Kempis

WHAT THE LAW SAYS THE IEP MUST CONTAIN

"A statement of the child's present levels of academic achievement and functional performance, including . . . how the child's disability affects the child's involvement and progress in the general education curriculum (i.e., the same curriculum as for non-disabled children); or . . . for preschool children, as appropriate, how the disability affects the child's participation in appropriate activities."

WHAT THE LAW MEANS

There's a reason this is the first required element of an IEP. The IEP Team can't know where they plan to go with the child's education if they don't know where they are starting. The Present Levels of Performance[9] is where the Team is setting the baseline of where the child stands with their skills at the start of an annual IEP, or any time the Team updates them with new information.

The whole purpose of special education is to reduce the impact a child's disability has on their education—academically and functionally. So in

> Over time, the present levels are reviewed at least annually so that growth, or lack of growth, can be measured.

order to "close the gap," you must first have a comprehensive understanding of the student's current skill levels—thus the term "present levels." So let's break down "academic achievement" and "functional performance."

Academic achievement refers to the academic subjects a child studies in school and the skills the student is expected to master in them. It includes concepts, knowledge, and skills in each of the content areas of the academic curriculum. Typical examples of academics include math, language arts (listening, speaking, reading, writing), science, and social studies.

Functional performance is generally understood as referring to skills or activities that are not considered academic in nature. It is used in the context of routine activities of everyday living. The range of functional skills is as varied as the individual needs of children with disabilities. The IEP Team must consider the impact the child's disability has on their ability to learn and do the kinds of things that typical, nondisabled children learn and do.

Gathering this information can come from a variety of assessment domains (psychological, cognitive, executive functioning,

---

9 This is frequently referred to as "PLOP" or "PLAAFP."

behavior, social, emotional, speech and language, life skills, etc.), observations, and input from educators and parents. It is critical to capture the child's strengths, as this will identify what helps the child learn. It's also important to determine what is interfering with the child's learning, the challenges or lagging skills that ultimately become the basis of an IEP goal.

The law goes on to say "or preschool children, as appropriate, how the disability affects the child's participation in appropriate activities," because the IDEA has set a different standard for preschoolers with disabilities. Preschool children are generally not involved in the "general education curriculum," but rather in activities with children of the same chronological age engaging in typical preschool pursuits like social activities, pre-academics, sharing time, independent play, listening skills, calendar, circle time, show-and-tell, etc.

WHAT PARENTS NEED TO KNOW

We believe the present levels are the first thing you should review when looking over your child's IEP after you have an IEP meeting because all goals flow directly from the present levels. If the impact of your child's disability is not in the present levels of performance, there won't be a goal to address your child's lagging skill(s).

It is not uncommon for parents and school personnel to disagree with what a child's present levels are. As an example, a parent may say that "Thomas is completely overwhelmed by school and is struggling, so much so that he has a meltdown when he comes home from school." But the school says, "He's fine at school, we don't see any signs of stress or struggle."

Perhaps a parent says that "Amara is not able to pronounce her 'r's' and she pronounces 'water' as 'watah.'" However, the school's speech and language pathologist, who has worked with her on articulation for years, says, "But she's now intelligible and it doesn't get in the way of her education."

> The fact is that the nature of school and home are different.

Children generally don't have the same level of academic demands placed on them at home. What you expect from your child at home is very different from what is expected at school. This explanation is often used as the basis for parents to be told why a lagging skill is not included in the PLOP/PLAAFP and that the concern won't ultimately turn into an IEP goal. You may end up disagreeing with the Team about whether this skill needs to be addressed. Don't be discouraged from speaking up and saying what you see, even if the Team doesn't agree with the fact that it should be captured in the present levels. If you do disagree, it's a good idea to ask for your Team to reflect your concerns in the IEP paperwork under the section that captures parent input and concerns.

When a school team explains that they don't see a concern at school, it's important to let them know that your child isn't generalizing the skill they are displaying at school to the home and community setting. To give an example, let's take a skill like "not leaving the group without permission." If the school team states that this skill is now mastered at school, but in your child's life in the rest of the world (home, the community, etc.) this remains a big problem, you need to explain that in order for a skill to truly be mastered, and therefore removed as an area of concern on the Present Levels, your child needs to be able to demonstrate it in more than one environment.

Please remember that your input is vital to creating the PLOP/PLAAFP. You are a required member of the IEP team, and your input should never be undervalued.

> If your child can't demonstrate a skill without the scaffolding of the support they get at school, it's not mastered.

If there is a suspected area of disability not included in your PLOP, let your team know that you would like your child evaluated in that area. Provide the team with examples of how you see your child struggling. Examples of areas of need can include:

- Academic skills (e.g., reading, writing, arithmetic)
- Activities of daily living (e.g., dressing, hygiene, cooking)
- Social (e.g., understanding emotions, getting along with others, manners and etiquette)
- Emotional (e.g., self-regulation, coping)
- Behavior (e.g., understanding and following school rules and other accepted behavioral norms)
- Sensory skills (e.g., reactions to environmental stimuli like noise, lights, and crowds)
- Communication (e.g., listening, conversation skills, speech and language)
- Mobility (e.g., ability to navigate the physical environment of the school and grounds, access to physical education, sports and playground)
- Health (e.g., understanding medical needs, sex education, addiction issues)
- Fine Motor (e.g., writing, fastening buttons, and scissor skills)
- Gross Motor (e.g., climbing stairs and accessing playground equipment)

It is the school district's legal responsibility to evaluate a child in *all* suspected areas of disability. So, this is where you are able to share any information you might be concerned about. Does your child's private therapist suspect anxiety or depression? Have you delicately mentioned your child has some of the same characteristics as your neighbor with autism? Does your child receive services because of an ADHD diagnosis, but you suspect a learning disability in writing, math, or reading?

Share this information with the Team and get it on the IEP record that this is a suspected area of disability and you would like for it to be evaluated.

> These gut feelings of yours matter. So do the concerns of an outside professional working with your child.

Only in this way can other potential areas of concern be included in the PLOP/PLAAFP. [10]

PARENT TAKEAWAY

The first thing we want you to think about when it comes to your child's IEP is the Present Levels of Academic Achievement AND Functional Performance. The PLOP is the foundation on which the IEP "house of goals" is built. Plippity, plappity, PLOP your way to building your child's IEP.

WHAT EDUCATORS AND RELATED PROFESSIONALS NEED TO KNOW

If you are a regular education teacher, special education teacher, reading teacher, school psychologist, school counselor, Board Certified Behavior Analyst, occupational therapist, physical therapist, or speech and language pathologist, or any number of other related educational professionals, you may be tasked with evaluating a child in order to determine their present levels of performance. It is your responsibility to ensure that it is accurate and complete.

Too often we see Present Levels that do not match up with IEP goals. As an example, there may be a goal for a challenging behavior that the student is exhibiting in school, but the behavior in question is not reflected in the Present Levels of Functional Performance. In this case, the IEP goals and the Present levels don't sync up.

Sometimes the parent might bring a lagging skill to your attention that you didn't prioritize or think should be included in the present levels.

> Remember, IEP goals flow directly from the present levels. So, if it's not in the PLOP, it shouldn't be a goal, and if you have an IEP goal for a skill, that area of deficit needs to be captured in the PLOP.

---

10 34 CFR 300.304

Please remember that parents are vital members of the team, and their input deserves your careful consideration. Also, we ask you to be mindful of the very different nature of school and home. School is far more "structured" than the average household and has a very con-

> The purpose of an IEP Team bringing together the home and the school perspectives is that students do not always neatly present the same way in one environment as they do in another. All perspectives are valuable.

crete schedule (most of the time). Also, many children very much avoid disappointing their teachers and becoming upset in front of peers but will come home and "let it all out" with tears, tantrums, and behavior.

It is possible that what you are seeing in school is very different from what the parents are seeing at home, and that both things can be true at the same time. It does not mean you or the parent is lying.

Finally, we want to end with an important word on how to interpret the required language of this section. A statement must be documented in the IEP regarding the child's "involvement and progress in the general education curriculum." Some school teams might interpret this to mean that a child only requires or qualifies for special education if they are not doing well academically. You might have heard explanations like, "Well, he gets good grades, so he isn't eligible for special education." Explanations like this are too common and too often wrongly disqualify students whose "functional performance" is the main basis for requiring special education. Remember, there are numerous categories for eligibility, and many of them are not "academic" in nature. Just because a student is "involved in and progressing" in the general education curriculum does not mean they are ineligible for special education services. Congress used the word "including" in this section of how the child's disability affects the child's involvement and progress in the general education curriculum. That doesn't "exclude" the child whose "functional performance" is the primary area of concern.

EDUCATOR TAKEAWAY

We've seen IEPs that don't quite get to the heart of what is preventing success for a child because the need has not been captured in the present levels. Sometimes this is because the area of concern was never evaluated. Or the area of disability was evaluated, but it wasn't prioritized to be included in the PLOP and thus is never developed as a goal. Too many times, we see the critical skills a child requires to be successful excluded from the IEP because the PLOP misses the boat. These critical skills go untaught year after year, too often resulting in poor outcomes. Don't miss the boat!

CHAPTER 2

MEASURABLE ANNUAL GOALS

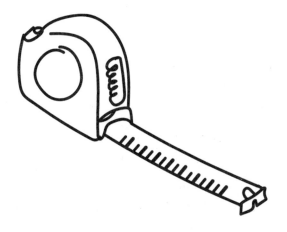

"Now some say it is unfair to hold disadvantaged children to rigorous standards. I say it is discrimination to require anything less—the soft bigotry of low expectations. . . ."
—George W. Bush, 1999 Speech on Education Policy

WHAT THE LAW SAYS

The legally mandated components of an IEP include:

"a statement of measurable annual goals including academic and functional goals, designed to meet the child's needs that result from the child's disability to enable the child to be involved in and make progress in the general education curriculum; and meet each of the child's other educational needs that result from the child's disability; a description of how the child's progress towards meeting the annual goals . . . will be measured and when periodic reports on the progress the child is making toward meeting the annual goal . . ."[11]

WHAT THE LAW MEANS

This portion of the IDEA's IEP requirements means that the IEP Team *must* include the Team's expectation of where the student will be one year from the start of the goal, assuming the student receives an appropriate program and makes meaningful progress. The goals must be developed at least once every single school year that the child is deemed eligible to receive an IEP.

> In *Endrew F. v. Douglas County School District* in 2017, the United States Supreme Court held that IEP goals should be "ambitious."

WHAT PARENTS NEED TO KNOW

Your child is in special education because they have lagging skills that need to be remediated. The purpose of special education is to develop skills, and this is your opportunity to ensure that the annual goals reflect specific skills that you want your child to learn in a year's time.

This requirement is for both academic *and* functional goals. To boil it down, education is about more than academics.

Academic achievement refers to the academic subjects a child studies in school and the skills the student is expected to master in each. These should align with the general education curriculum as much as possible.

Functional performance is generally understood as referring to skills or activities that are not considered academic; these are those skills we need to meet the demands of everyday life as independently as possible. The IEP Team must consider the impact the child's disability has on their ability to learn and do the kinds

---

11 20 USC 1414(d)(1)(A)(II)

of things that "typical," non-disabled children learn and do.

Goals drive services. The IEP services and accommodations that are going to be recommended are directly tied to the goals. The question the Team will ask after they develop the goals is "what services does this child need in

> "We do not believe it is necessary to include examples of functional skills in the regulations because the range of functional skills is as varied as the individual needs of children with disabilities."
>
> Commentary in the Federal Register (page 36661)

order to meet *these goals,* and how often do they need them?" If the goals themselves are *not* ambitious, you can be fairly sure that the services that will be recommended will not be robust. If the goals are not attainable, your child's time may be wasted for an entire year towards an unrealistic goal. If your child already has the skill that the goal is intended to have your child obtain, then they will be receiving services for something they already know how to do, rather than services that help them gain new strategies and learn something they do not yet know.

We will give you a specific example. Take a student who has dyslexia and is three grade levels behind their peers in reading. If the Team recommends an annual goal that in one year, the student will make one year's progress in reading, then where will that child be in one year if they have mastered that goal? Still three grade levels behind their peers in reading! That is not progress, let alone significant progress. The big picture goal should be to close the gap.

Your contribution to the goals is essential. All too often parents tell us that they don't get involved in contributing to the development of goals as the whole process makes their eyes gloss over. We understand why many parents leave goal writing entirely up to the educators—it's overwhelming. But we want you to pay special attention to them. We want you to give input into their development and understand how they are written.

When parents aren't mindful of them, they run the risk of having unmet goals on IEPs year after year with little progress, or goals can be written in a way that is so hard to understand, you don't really know what skills they are supposed to gain in a year. Some parents report to us, and we see this ourselves firsthand, that goals are written in a way that makes sense to the school team, but not to them. If your child has goals that don't make sense to you, we want you to ask the IEP Team to revise them with your input so they make sense to you.

Here's an easy way to think about a well-written goal. When you read the goal, ask yourself whether at the end of the year, if your child masters the goal as it is written, they will have a demonstrable and observable skill they don't have now. What will that skill be? If you can easily answer that question, that is a well-written goal.

Let's further break down the legally mandated components of IEP goals:

1. "a statement of measurable annual goals including academic and functional goals . . ."

This is extremely important. Note that this requirement is for both academic *and* functional goals. As a reminder, education is about more than academics. Many, many students who have disabilities are quite capable academically, but struggle with functional skills, or with coping skills, or with organizational skills, or with communication, etc. Also, the goals must be "measurable." A common acronym to ensure that goals are properly written is "SMART."

There are several different versions of "SMART" goals depending on who you ask. As an example, the "A" in SMART has frequently been defined as "achievable," or "attainable," or to stand for a goal that has "action words." We prefer changing the "A" in SMART to "ambitious" in keeping with

> **SMART** goals:
> Specific
> Measurable
> Ambitious
> Relevant
> Time-Bound

the Court's holding in *Endrew F.* Regardless of which particular acronym you prefer, they all get at essentially the same points: that IEP goals should be clear, well-written, and measurable.

2. "designed to meet the child's needs that result from the child's disability to enable the child to be involved in and make progress in the general education curriculum . . ."

This portion of the requirement of what goals must include is to make sure that when IEP Teams are developing goals, they are always focused on the fundamental expectation that students with disabilities are making progress in the curriculum that the school uses to teach *all* of the children within the school. After all, students who receive special education services are general education students first! The point of giving students with disabilities services, support, and accommodations is to enable them to learn in school alongside and with the same expectations as their nondisabled peers.

Required Members of the IEP Team

A. The public agency must ensure that the IEP Team for each child with a disability includes:
  1. The parents of the child;
  2. Not less than one regular education teacher of the child (if the child is, or may be, participating in the regular education environment);
  3. Not less than one special education teacher of the child, or where appropriate, not less than one special education provider of the child;
  4. A representative of the public agency who:
      (i). Is qualified to provide, or supervise the provision of, specially designed instruction to meet the unique needs of children with disabilities,
      (ii). Is knowledgeable about the general education curriculum, and
      (iii). Is knowledgeable about the availability of resources of the public agency;

    5. An individual who can interpret the instructional implications of evaluation results;

    6. At the discretion of the parent or the agency, other individuals who have knowledge or special expertise regarding the child, including related services personnel as appropriate;

    7. Whenever appropriate, the child with a disability.

B. Transition services participants.

    1. The public agency must invite a child with a disability to attend the child's IEP Team meeting if a purpose of the meeting will be the consideration of the postsecondary goals for the child and the transition services needed to assist the child in reaching those goals.

    2. If the child does not attend the IEP Team meeting, the public agency must take other steps to ensure that the child's preferences and interests are considered.

    3. To the extent appropriate, with the consent of the parents or a child who has reached the age of majority, the public agency must invite a representative of any participating agency that is likely to be responsible for providing or paying for transition services.

34 CFR 300.321

One easy way for you as a parent to ensure that this part of your child's rights is being honored in the development of the goals is to ask questions of the team as to where a student who does not have an IEP is expected to be in this skill area at this point in their education. This will give you a frame of reference. A regular education teacher is required at any IEP meeting where the student receives any portion of their programming in general education. This is a good person to ask in the meeting about expectations for children at this age and grade level.

As an example, a seventh grade student who has an IEP to address an attention deficit disorder has a proposed annual goal that they complete a task in the classroom 60 percent of the time with no more than one adult prompt. In order to know if this is a good goal, it is extremely useful to know what the expectations are for a student your child's age who does not have an IEP. A question like "what percentage of the time does the average 7th grader complete a task in the classroom without redirection?" will prove helpful. If the answer is "90 percent," then is the goal to have this student completing a task at 60 percent of the time at the end of the year ambitious? Is this closing the gap in the way this student is performing as opposed to their peers? And as importantly, where is your child performing now? If she is able to currently complete a task without redirection according to the data only 50 percent of the time, is only increasing it by 10 percent an appropriate goal for an entire year?

3. Goals are also required to "meet each of the child's *other* educational needs that result from the child's disability."
This seems fairly straightforward, but language matters and here the word we want you to re-read is "each." The goals are required to address *each* educational (reminder, not just "academic") need that results from your child's disability.

Some school teams come to the conclusion that if the student has access to the curriculum and is making progress in it, then all of the child's educational needs have been met. But the law does not end the analysis there, nor should you. We also want you to be mindful of the word "other" here. This means that in addition to goals that will enable the child to participate and make progress in the general education curriculum, the IEP goals must also address the student's "other" needs based on their present levels of academic and functional performance.

Now, in a perfect world this would be easy, but the reality is that there is a wide range of ability and disability in our world. For a student with a straightforward learning disability, it may be far easier to identify the academic goals for that student than for some students who are more significantly impacted by their disabilities. For some of these children, it is nearly impossible to address each and every one of their needs at the same time. You may have to prioritize those areas which concern you the most. That said, we never want you to feel you are having to choose from among several necessary skills for your child. They should each be addressed. We just ask you to be thoughtful about this at the various stages of your child's education.

4. Goals must also include "a description of how the child's progress towards meeting the annual goals . . . will be measured and when periodic reports on the progress the child is making toward meeting the annual goal . . ."
The IDEA requires that IEP goals include exactly how the Team will measure the goals, and how frequently progress towards the goals will be reported to the parents. The IDEA also requires that at a minimum, parents of students with IEPs need to receive a report on progress as frequently as parents of children who do not have IEPs get them. This means that every time the general education children get a report card, the children with IEPs are supposed to not only get their report cards, but an update on progress towards IEP goals.

It is really important that parents understand how their child's goals will be measured. Too frequently, the basis for progress monitoring is anecdotal (criteria like "observation" of progress as an example) and not necessarily based on hard data. Parents should make sure they understand how mastery will be determined and by which Team member or members. Is there a particular instrument or assessment that the teachers will be using to determine whether progress has been made? Has a baseline been established? If so, what is it? These are the types of questions you will want answered before agreeing to proposed goals.

PARENT TAKEAWAY

Goals are every bit as important as services, and in fact, the services your child gets and their frequency will be connected to the agreed-upon goals. Take the time to read them, review them in detail, ask questions, and provide your input on the proposed goals.

WHAT EDUCATORS AND RELATED PROFESSIONALS NEED TO KNOW

The very definition of an IEP by law includes the required elements of IEP goals. In other words, an IEP that does not include annual goals that:

- address the student's academic and functional skills, allow the student to make progress towards the general education curriculum;
- meet each of the child's other education needs that result from their disability;
- and state how they are to be measured and how frequently progress will be reported to the parents . . .

is *not* legally sufficient.

How goals are written matters a great deal. The expectation is that a student's services are based on what is necessary to master the annual goals. In addition, as a practical matter, poorly written goals frequently result in confusion on the part of the providers charged with implementing them.

Many special education teachers and related service providers are trained on writing IEP goals as they work toward their degrees. However, when they take a job in a particular school district, what frequently happens is their supervisors will provide them with additional information on how to write goals. Sometimes, this results in the educators getting out of the habit of checking to make sure the goals they are writing are in keeping with the law. It can become easy to be formulaic with IEP goals when you write many of them for many students, especially in this age where many software programs allow for "drop down menus" from which to choose goals. Please do not ever forget, however, that IEP goals are supposed to be *individualized* to meet this *particular* child's unique needs.

We strongly suggest that you try to write goals in a way that almost any parent can understand them. We can't tell you how often we have seen IEP goals proposed and implemented that are nearly impossible for an average person to understand. When we try to address this concern for the parents, we are frequently told "that's how we write them here at this school." This kind of a response is not only unlikely to result in a good understanding on the parents' parts of what you are trying to accomplish, it may even result in the parents stating that they disagree with the proposed goals simply because they don't understand them.

When writing IEP goals, in addition to asking yourself, "Does this goal include the federally required elements?" ask yourself a much more simple question: "Can someone who doesn't work in this school understand what I am hoping this child will be able to do a year from now if they master this goal?" If the answer is "no," then the parents in all likelihood do not know what you are proposing to accomplish.

Another question we wish more teachers would ask themselves before finalizing goals is whether these goals would be easily understood by a teacher if this child moved to another district or state. Can a new teacher on your team pick up the document and understand how to instruct the student based on that goal?

We chose the quote at the beginning of this chapter for a reason. Too often, our society in general and our schools in particular do not have high expectations for what students with disabilities can achieve. This is perhaps one of the biggest barriers to students with disabilities getting what they need in school. We must presume competence in our students who have IEPs, yes, but verify that we are not writing "empty" goals which don't result in true skills.

Be aware of your district's legal obligation to right the wrong of a poorly written goal. We realize that educators frequently "inherit" goals to work on with students that they did not actually write. Rather, the teacher from the prior year did, or sometimes an entirely different Team drafted them. We know from the look on their faces when an educator is unhappy with how an IEP goal is worded. Here's what you need to know: If a goal you have been asked to implement is not, in your view, in keeping with the law, or is otherwise fundamentally flawed in some way, it is not just your right to ask to reconvene the IEP Meeting or propose an IEP Amendment to change the flawed goal, it is the district's legal obligation to do so. One of the worst things a parent can discover at their child's Annual Review IEP Meeting is that an educator has been working on a goal all year that they didn't personally draft but don't think is appropriate. What the parent hears is that their child's precious time was wasted for a full year working on a poorly written goal that nobody bothered to change.

We gently ask teachers and providers to remember that while they usually have training that the parents of this child do not have, the parents have had the longest history with the student. If they are telling you that a proposed goal has been worked on for years without mastery, or if it is not ambitious enough to result in skill acquisition, they likely have a good reason to believe it. Establishing a family's priorities for their child's future should be a part of any IEP Team discussion, and the goals should reflect that fact.

EDUCATOR TAKEAWAY

Goals are required by law to have specific elements in order for them to be deemed sufficient. They should be easy for parents to understand, and measurable and specific enough that educators can implement them without reading the mind of the person who wrote them. They should be specific and reflect ambitious expectations of what skills the child will have in one year's time, and they should be changed as soon as possible if they do not comply with the law or expectations when written.

CHAPTER 3

PROGRESS MONITORING

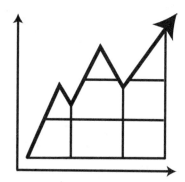

"A lack of transparency results in distrust and a deep sense of insecurity."
—Dalai Lama

WHAT THE LAW SAYS

The legally mandated components of an IEP include:

"... a description of how the child's progress towards meeting the annual goals described ... will be measured and when periodic reports on the progress the child is making toward meeting the annual goals (such as through the use of quarterly or other periodic reports, concurrent with the issuance of report cards) will be provided."[12]

---

12 20 USC 1414(d)(1)(A)(III)

WHAT THE LAW MEANS

Once a child has been determined to be eligible for an IEP, it is the task of the IEP Team to keep track of whether they are gaining skills. Just as schools regularly provide feedback to parents of children who do not have disabilities in the form of report cards and other information as to how their students are performing in school, the IDEA requires that progress towards the Annual Measurable Goals is maintained and shared with the parents of children who are receiving special education. Therefore, the IEP must specifically define how progress towards the goals will be measured, and how often and in what way it will be reported. How the student is performing in their identified areas of need must be written into the IEP document with a statement of how frequently the educators will document where the student's skill acquisition stands.

> Very frequently, IEP Teams report out on IEP progress at the same time they send report cards home for students who do not have IEPs. Certainly, every time report cards go out in a school, the team should be sending out progress towards IEP goals as well.

WHAT PARENTS NEED TO KNOW

One of the biggest disadvantages that parents of children with disabilities face as members of the IEP Team is that they are not in the school all day every day to observe how their child is doing in the way that the school team members are. This is one of the reasons why the IEP Team is required to let you know on a regular basis how your child is doing.

It can be very easy in the moment of the IEP Team Meeting to focus on the service hours, programs, and placement discussion rather than the "nitty gritty" of how details like progress monitoring are recorded into the IEP. However, you have a right to participate in determining the details of how you will be informed about your child's progress toward the goals. Do you want progress to be reported to you quarterly? Do you want monthly updates? While the team may not agree with your requests for how progress will be monitored, you are entitled to be part of the discussion on this topic. You don't want to find yourself learning that your child has made absolutely no progress towards an Annual Goal at the end of the year IEP Meeting, so staying on top of and reviewing those progress reports is essential.

As important as documenting how often you will be told about progress towards Annual Goals is agreeing upon HOW the progress will be measured. Too frequently, it is "anecdotal" rather than based on quantifiable data. For example, if your child has a goal to address learning to read, it is far less useful and reliable for you to be told every quarter that the teacher feels that he is keeping up in reading based on "teacher reports" than it is to know that in September they tested at an emerging first grade level, and in June that level remained the same.

We know that staying on top of each aspect of your child's IEP can be daunting, especially for parents who are not educators or related professionals. Don't feel the pressure to know all of the answers at the IEP Meeting. The document will be sent to you after the meeting and you should take the time

> Try to get into the habit of setting aside a solid chunk of uninterrupted time to review the entire IEP document when you receive it, preferably within a few days after the meeting. See "The Dreaded IEP Paperwork" chapter (p. 19).

you need to review it, in detail, and to be sure it reflects your understanding and agreement.

Another issue we have seen with progress monitoring is that the ways in which goals are measured is frequently dictated by forms designed by your school district or state with a list of fairly vague options. As an example, the IEP goal might have a "key" at the bottom that gives the educator the option to check one of the following boxes: "not introduced," "not achieved," "some progress," "satisfactory progress," "mastery," or our personal favorite: "other." If your IEP team wants to use "other" as a possible measure of progress, you need to be certain you know what they mean by it!

Unfortunately, sometimes a student's progress toward a goal is checked off as "satisfactory" each quarter until the last one, when it is suddenly either "mastered" or "not achieved." This is where your role as an informed and involved parent comes in. When you are getting your progress reports on the goals, read them, and ask questions if you are unclear.

As an example, your child has a fine motor goal to learn how to use a pair of scissors correctly and independently. However, when you see her attempt this at home, she is not able to cut with scissors without you physically helping her to do so. Yet, the report comes home from school that the occupational therapist has marked her with making satisfactory progress toward that goal. It could be that this is because the OT gives your child physical support when cutting. Does that mean this skill is independent? Probably not. However, it is also possible that your child is actually demonstrating the skill independently within the structured environment of a small related-service room at school but is distracted at home. The point is you won't know if you don't ask. A simple email to the teacher and OT noting that you aren't seeing this skill coming along satisfactorily at home and asking them to give you the data to support how they are measuring it will go a long way to making sure months don't go by without addressing the lack of progress.

PARENT TAKEAWAY

The IEP flows in a certain way: first establishing baseline through present levels, then developing measurable annual goals to address lagging skills, then monitoring progress towards those goals. Making sure you are comfortable with how the IEP reflects how those skills are going to be measured and when is crucial to ensuring your child doesn't fall further behind.

WHAT EDUCATORS AND RELATED PROFESSIONALS NEED TO KNOW

As with other required elements of an IEP, the very definition of an IEP by law includes a definition of progress monitoring. An IEP that does not contain a description of:

- How the child's progress towards meeting the annual goals will be measured; and
- When periodic reports on the progress the child is making toward meeting the annual goals will be provided is **not** legally sufficient.

As with many other aspects of the drafting of IEPs, it has become far too easy to rely on software programs and other "drop down menus" when developing a plan for progress monitoring. Frequently, educators are not even given much of a choice on this . . . local and state educational agencies simply tell you that you have to use their "system." However, remember that if you do not believe as a professional that the progress monitoring options available to you through that system will allow you to truly and accurately report on the goals, you can always ask how you can develop a different way of measuring progress.

If the best way that you think you can assess a student's progress is with a particular test or curriculum-based assessment, then take the time to explain that to the parents and memorialize it into the progress monitoring description. Unclear descriptions of how progress will be documented like "per teacher report" or "observation" are not

Parents frequently feel they have little idea what is actually happening in their child's special education and related-service time. Progress monitoring is one way to keep them informed, but it is not the only way. Many families welcome team meetings or other more frequent ways of staying informed. Those opportunities also can benefit you, as the parent might have some insight into why something you are doing is, or is not, working.

only unreliable descriptors for other educators, they are completely meaningless to parents.

Being clear with and getting input from a parent as to how a goal will be monitored will usually result in the parent being much more likely to understand and agree with how you are reporting progress. When they can see data and clear indicators of success, they will trust you more, even when they may not be observing that level of performance outside of school with their child. However, the reverse is also true. If the parents are not experiencing that their child is making meaningful progress, and your response is essentially that they are simply because you say it is so, you will have lost a great deal of credibility with them.

In addition, while it is statistically extremely rare that disagreements about special education progress will end up in litigation, it does happen. And when it does, it's usually the teachers, not the administrators, who have to testify and defend the programming. If you are ever in such a situation, believe us, you will want to feel confident that you can defend the level of progress recorded.

We greatly appreciate and understand the enormous obligations that rest on the shoulders of teachers when developing IEPs, and some of these details may seem to matter little. However, to a parent who is trying to understand how their child is doing in school, especially if their child is unable to share much detail with them directly, these progress reports are vital.

Finally, there is no shame in acknowledging that a student is not making progress towards the goals you thought were reasonable when written. Too frequently teachers keep working at a goal all year that is just not coming along. If it's clear that a goal is not going to be mastered by the end of the year, you have a right and an obligation to either reconvene the IEP Meeting to discuss revising the goals or services, or to suggest that the IEP be amended to address the concerns.

EDUCATOR TAKEAWAY

The law requires that educators be transparent and accountable when it comes to progress towards IEP goals. The manner in which goals will be monitored must be included in the IEP itself. Detailed and honest reporting on whether a student is actually meeting those goals is essential not only for a trusting relationship with the parents of a student, but to ensure that the child is actually receiving the appropriate education to which they are entitled by law.

CHAPTER 4

SUPPORTS AND SERVICES

"One of the most important gifts a parent can give a child is the gift of accepting that child's uniqueness."

—Fred Rogers

WHAT THE LAW SAYS

An IEP must include "A statement of the special education and related services and supplementary aids and services, based on peer-reviewed research to the extent practicable, to be provided to the child, or on behalf of the child, and a statement of the program modifications or supports for school personnel that will be provided to enable the child . . . to advance appropriately toward attaining the annual goals; to be involved in and make progress in the general education curriculum; and to participate in extracurricular and other nonacademic activities; and to be educated and participate with other children with disabilities and nondisabled children."

WHAT THE LAW MEANS

In the simplest of terms, an IEP is designed to teach a child skills that they currently do not have. These weaknesses are documented to have adversely impacted the student's involvement and progress in their education—academically and/or functionally. The IEP goals are written for a full year, and designed for the skill to be mastered by the end of that year. The plan for how the Team intends to get the child to the point where they have met the goal in a year is largely documented in the description of what services and supports the student requires in order to achieve their goals.

Individualized supports and services are supposed to be designed to help the student make meaningful progress toward their annual goals, and to be involved in and make progress in the general education curriculum.

The law goes on to say ". . . and to participate in extracurricular and other non-academic activities; and to be educated and participate with other children with and without disabilities."

What the law means here is that we want to make sure that children with disabilities are not excluded from any of the activities that their typically developing peers are involved in, including school-sponsored activities that take place beyond the traditional school day hours or other activities like sports, plays, musicals, musical performances, etc.

This portion of the law means that the IEP paperwork must include statements (or sections in the IEP paperwork) that detail how the IEP will be carried out directly by educators and related service providers.

WHAT PARENTS NEED TO KNOW

Please know that a child's need for supports and services are sometimes underestimated by school professionals due to limited resources. Educators and related services professionals might be under a great deal of pressure to "downplay" what supports and services your child requires due to the directives they have received from administrators or other decision makers whose job it is to be mindful of resources and budgets. We certainly appreciate this, but decisions on what your child requires should be based on their needs.

When you participate in the development of your child's IEP, ask questions. Try to understand why a particular service recommendation is made. If the occupational therapist says, "I'm recommending a half hour a week of OT," ask why this amount. Commonly, the services' hours are chosen due to scheduling blocks or a provider's schedule rather than the needs of this individual child. If your child was always getting forty-five-minute sessions in elementary school, and now in middle school the team is suddenly recommending thirty-seven minutes, is that because your child's needs have changed? Or is a "period" in middle school thirty-seven minutes?

> The IEP should detail the specialized instruction (special education), related, and supplemental services your child requires.

> You have the right to disagree with the providers' recommendations!

In addition to specifying what special education, supplementary, and related services your child will require, this portion of the IEP also must document how your child is able to access the general education environment in their school, *including* non-academics like athletics, clubs and organizations, and school events.

For students who struggle in school, sometimes the only time during their day they feel capable is during "non-academics" like sports, arts, and activities. Also, if they are receiving a tremendous amount of "pull-out" from the general education environment as part of their IEP, these "extracurriculars" are some of the most meaningful times they have to interact socially with their peers.

Too frequently, IEP Teams overlook the services a student requires to be able to benefit from the general education environment. Be sure not to let that happen.

> Never forget that your child is a "regular education" student first! If they need services or supports to participate in non-academics, that should be spelled out in the IEP.

PARENT TAKEAWAY

As a general rule, students with disabilities are general education students first, and they are entitled to have supports, services, and modifications in place that enable them to advance towards their goals, and to participate in the non-academics and extracurriculars available to all students. Be sure you understand what individualized supports and modifications are being provided to your child through their IEP.

WHAT EDUCATORS AND RELATED PROFESSIONALS NEED TO KNOW

We know that resources are typically stretched thin in special education. As educators, you rely on your colleagues to help you to fulfill all the needs of your students and their individual needs prescribed in their IEPs.

Due to limited resources, we know that you are sometimes put in the position of making recommendations for supports and services that are less than what you believe a student really needs to make an appropriate rate of progress toward their IEP goals. Related service providers are especially put in tough positions, as many times they are the only person with that certification in the building, and they are being asked to meet the needs of a growing population of students with disabilities.

It can become very easy to write IEP goals based on what you are planning to do differently for this particular child than you do for other students, but it's important to document the things you do for all your charges as well. As an example, if you are a teacher who makes sure to spend an hour a week talking with other providers on your team, regardless of how many students you have on your caseload, that time really should be reflected in the IEP if this child cannot receive an appropriate program unless the team is consulting with one another weekly.

> You may need help too! This portion of the IEP must include a statement of what supports the school personnel may require in order to provide the child with an appropriate program. If you feel you will need the consultation time of another professional in order to carry out your tasks for this child, ask that it be included in this portion of the IEP.

Similarly, if in working with a student you have realized that you are actually spending more time with them, or with other members of the team discussing them, than the IEP currently calls for, it needs to be changed in the IEP. We frequently hear educators say things like, "It's on the IEP for an hour a week

> An IEP travels with a child if they move to a new town or state. Ask yourself: If this child moved tomorrow and a new team picked up the child's IEP, would they really know how much we are doing? Are the services and supports reflective of what is actually happening and what the student genuinely needs?

but honestly, we are probably spending closer to two hours on it." While it's laudable that a teacher is going "above and beyond," what that statement really means is that the child's current performance requires the two hours of service. So that should be documented in the IEP and changed to reflect what they are actually requiring.

This portion of the IEP is not designed only to document the academic and educationally related services, modifications, and supports the student is receiving in the classroom, but also to outline what the student requires to participate in the general education environment, *including* extracurriculars.

If the student in question is athletically capable, as an example, but will need an adult to be able to participate in the sport because in school they need a 1:1 para for safety reasons, they may need the IEP to spell out that a 1:1 should attend practice with them. If a student is deaf, but also a talented actor, it may be that the IEP needs to delineate some modifications of that activity so that the student is not denied access to the non-academic part of the school experiences that their nondisabled peers are able to participate in.

> Please take care to think in advance about non-academic and extracurricular experiences for students with disabilities, and what services and supports they would need to participate. For some children, this is the only part of their school experience where they get to socialize and feel capable.

The population of students with disabilities has been growing rapidly. We understand that you might feel pressure from administrators to underestimate what you know your students really need for support and services. We know of far too many instances where teachers have been directed to keep their recommendations in line with the school district's resources versus what they truly believe the student requires.

> Federal and even many state laws protect educators from being disciplined by their employers for advocating for the rights of individuals with disabilities.

This may be a bit lofty for us to imagine, but we would like to see a world in which educators and related service providers are free to recommend what supports and services that they truly believe their students need for their IEPs.

We certainly don't want to jeopardize your job,[13] but we encourage you to speak your truth and make the recommendations for supports and services you genuinely believe need to be in place

---

13 Indeed, we explain the institutional pressure many teachers are under in our first book in a chapter called "Teachers Need to Eat, Too."

for this child based on your professional expertise. You know the children you are working with far better than some person who happens to be chairing the meeting, but who has never met them. Part of your role as an educator is to educate the other adults on the IEP Team about what this child genuinely requires, and federal law mandates that the details of those special education and related services, and supplementary supports, are documented in the IEP.

EDUCATOR TAKEAWAY

In addition to being prepared to document the services, modifications, and supports that the students you are working with require in this part of the IEP, this is your opportunity to also express what YOU as an educator need in order to be able to be successful in working with a child. The key to this section for you is the language "supports for school personnel" to implement the IEP.

CHAPTER 5

EXPLANATION OF REMOVAL

"Part of the problem is that we tend to think that equality is about treating everyone the same, when it's not. It's about fairness. It's about equity of access."

—Judith Heumann

WHAT THE LAW SAYS

The legally mandated components of an IEP include "an explanation of the extent, if any, to which the child will not participate with nondisabled children in the regular class and activities. . . ."[14]

---

14 20 USC 1414(d)(1)(A)(V)

WHAT THE LAW MEANS

It is sometimes easy to forget that the core underpinning of the IDEA, from a historical perspective, was the segregation and exclusion of children with disabilities from our public schools. Prior to the passage of the IDEA, students with disabilities had NO federal entitlement to attend public school, let alone was there any standard for what level of education they should receive. For this reason, there are numerous portions of the federal law designed to ensure that students with disabilities are not discriminated against simply because they require special education and related services, and that the removal of students with IEPs from the general education setting is only done when absolutely necessary. For this reason, the IEP itself must document

> "Before the date of enactment of the Education for All Handicapped Children Act of 1975, the educational needs of millions of children with disabilities were not being fully met because . . . the children did not receive appropriate educational services; the children were excluded entirely from the public school system and from being educated with their peers; undiagnosed disabilities prevented the children from having a successful educational experience; or the lack of adequate resources within the public school system forced families to find services outside of the public school system." – IDEA, Congressional Findings

why and how (the "explanation") the student will be removed from participation in the regular classroom and other activities in which they would otherwise be learning and participating alongside their nondisabled peers.

WHAT PARENTS NEED TO KNOW

Your child is entitled to *both* receive the special education and related services they require *and* to be treated as a general education student *first*. Unfortunately, very frequently, parents are asked as part of the development of the IEP to sacrifice their child's participation in the mainstream school environment and regular classroom in order to get their services.

By requiring the IEP Team to document the extent to which a student will not participate in the regular classroom and how and whether and for what activities they will be removed from their peers, Congress sought to ensure that the IEP Team, including parents, were thoughtful and deliberate, and that IEP Team *must* explain why they have made that recommendation.

While the IDEA does contemplate that for some students at various points in their education, a "more restrictive" program may be necessary, the mandate is for the program to be provided in the "least restrictive environment" that is appropriate to meet the student's needs. That is your child's right. We should always presume competence, and the default should be that the student with disabilities attends the school and classrooms they would attend if they didn't have an IEP.

We always like to explain that the LRE is a continuum, and that an IEP must be appropriate regardless of what level of restrictiveness the placement contemplates. Some school teams might argue that it would be "too restrictive" to take a child out of the general education setting; and that is generally true, especially if they did so without attempting to provide the student with the supplementary aids and supports necessary to be successful in general education. It's important to be able to discuss in which environment the student would be most available for learning and in which they would make the best rate of progress. For some students, the general education setting can be a restrictive environment because they are not available to learn or make an appropriate rate of progress.

> Unfortunately, many recommendations come out of IEP meetings which are reflections not of what the individual child requires, but rather a reflection of how special education programs have been set up in that particular school. The question should not be "Where do you provide that service?"; the question should be "What does this child require and how can we provide it without removing the child from the environment they would be in if they did not have a disability?"

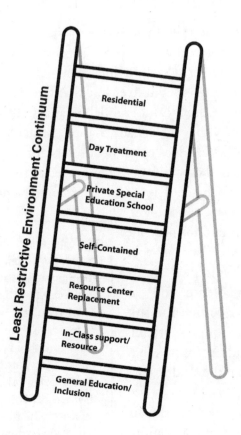

The LRE includes a wide variety of options for placement including:

Home instruction
Hospital setting
Residential placements
Private special education schools outside of the district
Separate special education locations within a school district
Self-contained
Pull-out support/services in resource room
Before or after school tutoring
Push-in to general education support /services (specialist in the general education classroom)
General education (inclusion)

If you believe that your child benefits from being in the general education environment more than the IEP Team does, you should be having discussions with them about how the support and services can be provided without removal from that environment. Does a paraprofessional need to be added to the IEP to assist the child in being able to be in the regular classroom for more of the day? Can a related service provide "push in" to the general education environment and work on developing skills there, or in a non-academic or unstructured time that involves your child's peers, rather than everything being a "pull-out" model?

As with all aspects of the development of the IEP, the explanation of time that your child will not be participating with their peers is a topic on which your input and opinion is required to be considered. It is also something that is frequently misunderstood. Many parents do not realize, as an example, that in some schools (particularly after elementary school), the "schedule" of the school is such that if a child is receiving special education, they are "giving up" participation in an educational opportunity that they might otherwise attend and enjoy: a foreign language; an "elective" like chorus or band; a "homeroom," etc. Make sure you are asking questions about how the special education and related services that are being proposed impact your child's ability to interact with and be educated alongside their peers.

PARENT TAKEAWAY

Generally speaking, the IEP Team will propose special education and related services first, and later in the meeting they will fill out this required portion of the IEP that delineates how much of the student's time will be away from nondisabled peers in the regular classroom. Be careful to ask about the impact of that time in the general education environment before you have agreed to the proposed services. And always be mindful of the balance between the benefit of intensive services and interaction with nondisabled peers, and where to strike that balance in your child's program.

WHAT EDUCATORS AND RELATED PROFESSIONALS NEED TO KNOW

The IDEA and most of the cases which interpret it hold the entitlement of students with disabilities to be educated alongside their nondisabled peers very seriously, as they should. Congress did not open the doors of public education to children who require IEPs only to isolate them in self-contained classes and prohibit them from their right to attend regular classes in the program and school they would otherwise attend if they did not have special education needs. So by law the IEP must specifically document an explanation of any removal from the regular classroom and activities which will result in the student being educated without their nondisabled peers.

Special education students are general education students first. As Anne Donnellan stated in 1984, "the criterion of the least dangerous assumption holds that in the absence of conclusive data, educational decisions ought to be based on assumptions that, if incorrect, will have the least dangerous effect on the likelihood that students will be able to function independently as adults." In other words, when making educational decisions for students, we should first look at whether the intervention and supports we are providing them are successful, rather than assuming that any lack of success or progress the child is making is a result of their inherent disability.

When you approach the development of the IEP from the viewpoint that students with special education needs should be educated with their nondisabled peers "to the maximum extent appropriate," you will not only be following the law, you will also be teaching that student and all of the other students in the regular classroom that individuals with disabilities are valuable members of their schools. Students with disabilities should not have to "prove" they can be in the mainstream, nor should their IEP be written in such a way as to have the child "earn" their way into the regular classroom or general education environment. That is their right.

ALWAYS Presume Competence.

It is also important to be extremely thoughtful and individualized in how the recommendation for services will impact the amount of time the student will be removed from the mainstream. The fact that a more restrictive classroom or program exists in a particular school does not necessarily mean that this is where we place all students who struggle in school. This is an especially common assumption made for students whose behavior impacts them in the general education setting. Ironically, the reflexive decision to remove students from their peers often has the exact opposite result, and frequently teams will see a student's maladaptive behaviors spike when they are isolated in a more restrictive environment for some part of their day.

EDUCATOR TAKEAWAY

By requiring an explanation of removal from the regular education environment as part of the mandated components to an IEP, Congress was reinforcing one of the cornerstone tenets of the IDEA: meaningful inclusion of students with disabilities in their schools. This is not just a box that has to be checked off in the IEP paperwork, but rather, a deliberate and important discussion that involves the entire team.

CHAPTER 6

STATE/DISTRICT-WIDE TESTING

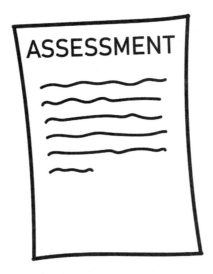

"If my future were determined just by my performance on standardized tests, I wouldn't be here. I guarantee you that."

—Michelle Obama

WHAT THE LAW SAYS

One of the legally mandated components of an IEP is:

a statement of any individual appropriate accommodations that are necessary to measure the academic achievement and functional performance of the child on state and district wide assessments . . . and if the IEP Team determines that the child shall take an alternate assessment on a particular state or district wide assessment of student achievement, a statement of why: the child cannot participate in the regular assessment; and why the particular alternate assessment selected is appropriate for the child.[15]

WHAT THE LAW MEANS

If a school district or state is conducting assessments for all students in the district or state, then the IEP has to reflect whether this student requires accommodations in order to participate in that testing in order to determine their academic and functional performance. What those accommodations are needs to be spelled out in the IEP. In addition, if the IEP Team determines that

> The IDEA specifically mandates that: "All children with disabilities are included in all general state and district-wide assessment programs . . . with appropriate accommodations and alternate assessments where necessary and as indicated in their respective individualized education programs."[1]
>
> 1 20 USC 1412(a)(16)(A)

the child should *not* take the standard testing that nondisabled students are taking, and instead take an "alternate" test, the IEP must explain why the IEP Team has determined that the child can't take the standard test, and why the alternate test chosen by the IEP Team is appropriate for this child.

WHAT PARENTS NEED TO KNOW

The topic of state and district-wide testing is almost always a hot one for those interested in education. Many parents and educators feel that our educational system has become overly focused on these tests, with many complaining that instead of teaching children to learn, we have become a country that "teaches to the test." These debates will likely rage on for many years to come.

---

15 20 USC 1414(d)(1)(A)(VI)

However, regarding your child with an IEP, there are pros and cons to having your child participate in this type of testing, which we will get to in a moment.

What is important to understand is *why* Congress has mandated that students with IEPs participate in this type of testing along with their nondisabled peers. First, it is helpful to always look at the IDEA from a civil rights perspective. Equal educational opportunities are a civil right, as is the right to be free from discrimination based on disability. When passing the IDEA, Congress wanted to be sure that students with disabilities were not excluded from the types of testing that local and state educational agencies use to monitor the quality of the education in their town or state. If you think about it, that makes sense. It would not be surprising if a school system preferred to exclude students who struggle with academics from their statistics on how they are performing in educating students.

You should also understand that state and district-wide testing is typically not "standardized" in the same way that individualized testing that should be used in the process of evaluating your child for IEP purposes is. The kinds of testing that many IEP Teams use to determine if a student has a disability (e.g., IQ testing, academic achievement testing, speech and language assessments, rating scales, etc.) are usually published by companies which have made sure the tests are "normed" across many thousands of students over many years, with periodic updates to the forms, and should be very reliable if they are chosen and administered properly by the IEP Team for your child. That is not the case with most of the district and statewide tests that are being used throughout the US. They do have some reliability in terms of assessing how a particular educational *system* is doing, but they are not nearly as focused on how an *individual child* is performing.

That said, there are some very good reasons why you want your child to participate in district and statewide testing. First, from a social/emotional perspective, and the lens that we always presume competence and inclusion, when your child's whole class or grade or school is taking a test, you don't necessarily want them to be removed from the group experience. Indeed, even some students who require accommodations to take the test bristle at the idea of being removed from the class with their peers.

Second, whether your child takes the test with accommodations or not, the outcome can be informative for you and the

> Be cautious about agreeing to an "alternate" district or statewide test for your child. Typically, these are very, very different from the skills being tested for the other students and may significantly inflate how your child's performance on the test looks.

IEP Team as to whether your child is keeping up with the other students in their class/grade/school/district/state. If you keep being told by your child's school that she is doing just fine, but you have your doubts, and the district-wide or state testing comes back and demonstrates that your child is in the bottom fifth of her school, it may verify some of those concerns. This is especially true if you note regression over time on the comparison between your child and the rest of the students taking the test.

You will want to know whether your state or district's testing has any impact on any decision-making regarding individual children, or it is being maintained solely to assess how the district or state is measuring up as an educational system. In other words, does your child's performance on the testing matter in any way? Does it dictate whether they are eligible for "gifted" programming? Does it impact class placement for any honors or remedial tracks moving forward? Does it have any role in determining who is eligible for certain types of diplomas, or whether your child will graduate on time? These are all important questions to ask *before* you are asked to agree on the testing, the accommodations, and whether an alternate assessment is necessary.

The discussion about which accommodations your child might need for district and statewide testing should be a robust one, although unfortunately in our experience it tends to be one of the last agenda items on an IEP Team's list and frequently "rushed through" at the tail end of the meeting. Try to avoid this.

Just like every other aspect of the IEP, the accommodations for state and district-wide testing should be individualized. As an example, if your child has a language-based learning disability which impacts how quickly they can read, the team may determine that a reasonable accommodation for him would be to have an adult "reader" to read him the questions. Obviously,

> A tip: in advance of your child's Annual Review IEP meeting, try to find out whether the current or coming school year will include district or statewide testing (some districts and States test every other year or even less frequently rather than annually) so that you can be sure to ask for time to discuss any necessary accommodations for the testing.

however, you wouldn't want them to have that accommodation in the portion of the test that assesses his reading skills. Or, if your child requires services due to significant attention difficulties, a separate, quiet setting for the test may make sense. Ask what options are available for accommodations so you can weigh in on what seems to be the right balance between making sure your child is not being excluded from this testing but, at the same time, their academic and functional performance are being accurately measured, rather than their frustration with a test.

Finally, there are some students who, due to significant disabilities, will require an alternate test. Make sure, however, you have an understanding of what that alternate test entails as compared with your child's peers, and whether it is appropriate for your child. You should check with your school or state as to whether an "opt out" option is available, should you choose.

PARENT TAKEAWAY

In general, school systems are mandated to include students with IEPs in the testing they administer to all children within the district or state. However, your child may require and be entitled to accommodations in order to participate effectively and in order for the results of the testing to have any meaning for your child. Be sure to have a meaningful discussion about this at your child's IEP Team, because this is a required component to the document.

WHAT EDUCATORS AND RELATED PROFESSIONALS NEED TO KNOW

An IEP by law requires that a statement be included which addresses district and statewide testing. That statement must address and document whether there are any necessary individualized accommodations for the Student on such testing, and if so, what they are. In addition, if the IEP Team determines that this student's disabilities are so impactful that even significant accommodations will not result in an accurate measure of the child's academic and functional performance, and that an alternate test is required, then the IEP MUST describe:

- o Why the child cannot participate in the regular testing with accommodations *and*
- o Why the team chose the particular alternate test for this student.

If these factors are not documented in the IEP, it is *not* legally sufficient.

This aspect of the IEP discussion, in our experience, is one of the topics that doesn't receive as much discussion and attention as it requires. While educators answer this question for students all the time, try to avoid brushing it over into a box that gets checked at the end of the meeting.

This is another area where we should presume competence. Look at the answer to this question just like you would consider whether a program or placement is too restrictive. Think of it as a continuum that way. Start with the assumption that the student can take this test along with their classmates, just like their classmates. Next, ask whether a simple accommodation would allow the student to perform adequately on the test. If more accommodations are needed, then discuss those with the parents and team. And always be sure to keep in mind WHAT the particular test is testing. Providing an accommodation for a student that is essentially removing any real information from the results of the test (e.g., giving a student with disability a calculator for a test that is measuring math calculations) is not

Alternate tests are listed in the Statute as requiring an explanation if recommended, and the standard for choosing alternate testing is that the student CANNOT participate in the regular testing with accommodations. It should be a recommendation treated as the exception, not the rule.

appropriate, unless it's a tool or support that their nondisabled peers are getting as well.

We always urge educators to be transparent with parents at the IEP Meeting about their concerns, but also the impact that some of the decisions being made have on the child *and* their future education. Many parents have no idea whether district or state-wide testing has any consequence to a particular child depending on how they perform on it. In many cases, it has absolutely no impact on the child or their education, and is only used by the school, local educational agency, or state to measure how their students in general are performing.

If, however, there are ways in which the results of the testing are going to impact educational opportunities for the child or have other consequences, we strongly suggest that you inform parents of this when discussing any necessary accommodations or alternate testing.

Finally, we want you to know that we understand how incredibly frustrating the pressure of more and more testing of this kind puts on educators. Many feel, and rightly so, that the testing consumes an inordinate amount of time, taking away from instruction, and does not really accurately indicate the quality of the education or the teachers who are providing it. We feel you. That said, just as with all aspects of the law, the IDEA is fundamentally a Civil Rights Act, and we don't want to exclude students with disabilities from activities all of their peers participate in, even if those activities are poor choices.

EDUCATOR TAKEAWAY

The documentation and discussion around whether and how a student will participate in district and statewide testing is a required and essential element of the IEP. It should be a thoughtful discussion with the parents on whether and how the child's disabilities will be factored into the testing so that the results are as accurate a reflection of the student's academic and functional performance as possible.

CHAPTER 7

WHEN, WHERE & HOW OFTEN

"Success is the sum of details."
—Harvey S. Firestone

WHAT THE LAW SAYS

The IDEA requires that an IEP includes a section that documents "the projected date for the beginning of the services and modifications described . . . and the anticipated frequency, location and duration of those services and modifications."[16]

WHAT THE LAW MEANS

IEPs are required to specifically state when the services and modifications[17] being proposed for the student will start, how

---

16 20 USC 1414(d)(1)(A)(VII)

17 The terms "modifications" and "accommodations" are not actually synonyms. They are, however, frequently used interchangeably. This section of the IEP includes reference to "modifications" rather than accommodations. "Accommodations" are referenced in the Statute under the statement of special

often they will occur, where, and for how long. To make it even more simple:

Projected Date: When will these services and modifications start?

Frequency: How many times a day, week, month, etc. is the service in effect?

Location: Where are these services and modifications taking place?

Duration: How long will this service or modification last?

> IEPs must be in effect at the beginning of the school year: "At the beginning of each school year, each local educational agency, state educational agency, or other state agency, as the case may be, shall have in effect for each child with a disability in the agency's jurisdiction, an individualized education program."[1]
>
> 1 20 USC 1414(d)(2)(A)

WHAT PARENTS NEED TO KNOW

After the IEP Team has determined the student's Present Levels of Academic Achievement and Functional Performance and developed goals, at some point they need to address what services and accommodations the child will require. The federal law requires that the IEP itself document when, where, and how often those services and modifications will occur.

This is a classic example of a phrase we use often: "the devil is in the details."

Why did Congress insist that this be included in the required elements of an IEP? Several reasons. First, how could the educators possibly know how to implement the IEP if this were not

---

education and related services section, found and described in this book in Chapter 4: Supports and Services. There are whole articles, chapters, and books on this subject, but a simple way to look at the difference between the two terms is this: modifications are changes in what the individual student is expected to produce or learn as compared with the rest of the class or group; accommodations are changes to the educational environment to ensure that the individual student can have access to the same content, materials, and opportunities as their nondisabled peers.

specified? Keep in mind, as an example, that very frequently the team of educators drafting an IEP for the following school year will not be the same team of providers who need to implement it. Also, what if a family moved from one state to another? How would the receiving team know what services the student was getting without this documentation?

Next, parents need to be aware of what is being proposed in order to consent to the IEP. Simply saying, "We are going to give James speech and language services" is not sufficient. How many hours a week will he get? There is a big difference between fifteen minutes of speech and language services and two hours. Where will it take place? Is this service a "push in" to the classroom, where the Speech Pathologist facilitates language for him in the general education environment, or is he being pulled out into a related service room for 1:1 instruction? When is it going to start? Right away? At some point in the future? And how long is the proposed service or modification proposed to be in effect?

> As noted in chapter 9, the IEP must also include a description of how much time the student will not participate with nondisabled children. Sometimes doing the math on the hours indicated in that section don't make sense if the service locations are as discussed . . . double and triple check this!

This part of the development of the IEP is required, as with all aspects of an IEP, to be individualized for your child. However, unfortunately, more often than we would like, we hear teams basing service hours and delivery location not on the unique needs of the child, but rather, on the schedule in that particular school, or the availability of the providers. It is very important that you are trying to ascertain why your team is proposing the particular services and modifications they are recommending. What about your child and how they are learning, progressing, or not is impacting the delivery of the supports?

There are a few ways that you can get a sense of whether the services and modifications being proposed for your child are in fact based on a true belief of what she requires, or something else, through comments made in the IEP meeting itself. If, as an example, when it gets to recommending hours, the recommendation for the hours of resource room support are two sessions, forty-three minutes a week for math; two sessions, forty-three minutes a week for reading; one session, forty-three minutes for executive functioning skills, you can be pretty sure that the length of the periods in that school are . . . drum roll . . . forty-three minutes! While we are not opposed to a plan that avoids disruption for a student and educators by aligning services with the schedule of the school, where we get frustrated is when the approach is inflexible in that regard. If you have a recommendation from a trusted professional that your child needs a minimum of an hour a week of a type of service, and instead forty-three minutes a week are being recommended, it may seem like a minor difference. But in a typical school year, that adds up to 680 minutes, or 11.33 hours of time difference. That is not insignificant.

> Don't forget, in addition to writing down where and when services are to be in effect, this section must also include the same information for modifications. You may or may not want to have modifications in all environments or parts of your child's day, so be sure you know when they are in effect and where. This is especially important for "modified grades," meaning your child is not being graded the same way on their report card/grades as their nondisabled peers.

Another way that you may be able to tell if the recommended services and modifications are indeed individualized for your child is whether the person who is tasked with providing them starts discussing their own schedule or availability when asked to propose time. If you believe your child needs Physical Therapy every day in school, and the PT says, "I'm only at this school on Tuesdays, so I recommend one time a week for thirty minutes" that definitely sounds like the recommended service hours are not based on your child's needs!

Many parents learn about the availability, or limitations, on services and support in their child's school or district by talking to other parents of children who have IEPs. That can be a valuable source of information, such as finding out that the district has recently lost a school psychologist who took another job, and suddenly hearing at your IEP Meeting that the counseling your child was getting from a school psychologist on their IEP is no longer being recommended. However, please know that sometimes parents either make assumptions based on what they hear from other parents, or don't know some pivotal facts about the other parent's child that would very much influence why that person was offered something that you weren't. Remember, the I in IEP stands for "individualized"!

Finally, knowing the details of when, where, and how long an IEP service or modification is being recommended is essential to enable you to meaningfully participate in the development of your child's IEP. Especially as your child moves along in their education into middle and high school, special education services and modifications can interfere with other class schedules and impact your child's ability to take certain electives, etc. The response to your concern in this regard will likely be something along the lines of "there are only so many hours in the day." We want you to be able to state why you don't agree that your child should have to sacrifice participation in the general education opportunities in exchange for receiving their necessary special education and related services. Problem-solve around this with your team, but only if you really understand the details of when, where, and how often the services and modifications are being proposed for by the IEP Team.

PARENT TAKEAWAY

We want you to always be vigilant in understanding what is being proposed by your child's IEP Team, but perhaps nowhere is it more important that you really focus on the details than when it comes to how the program is going to be delivered, in detail. Actually, we lied, it's all important, but really, this part is where the rubber meets the road!

WHAT EDUCATORS AND RELATED
PROFESSIONALS NEED TO KNOW

To even start to be legally sufficient, an IEP must include the details of the start date, frequency, location, and duration of services, *and* modifications being proposed.

This means you should come to the IEP meeting prepared with your proposals, but with the flexibility to engage in the necessary consideration of the input of the parent, and the discussion with the team, which may change your mind on what the student requires. Too often in our experiences, educators are "stuck" on the hours or modifications they walked into the meeting expecting to recommend. This is not only frustrating to parents when they

Parents are federally required IEP Team members, and must be assured of their role in the development of the IEP. The IDEA's procedural safeguards specifically note that they have the right to ". . . participate in meetings with respect to the identification, evaluation, and educational placement of the child, and the provision of a free appropriate public education to such child, and to obtain an independent educational evaluation of the child." If it is clear that the decisions about services and placement were made without them and in advance of the IEP Meeting, a finding of unlawful predetermination could be made.

are met with a "closed mind" about possible changes, but also can be interpreted as "predetermination" of the outcome of the IEP Meeting.

It may feel as if we are sending you mixed messages: on the one hand we are telling you to be prepared to make recommendations on service hours, location and duration, as well as start date, and on the other hand we are warning you about being deemed to have made up your mind just because you came in prepared. We want you to be prepared and have in fact found that a conversation with the parent in advance to go over your thoughts about the IEP can be very effective in giving them time to process your ideas, and may even result in them agreeing with you once they have done so. The key is not to have it "set in stone" in your mind or in fact before the IEP Meeting.

Things to avoid that give the impression of predetermination of services, supports, modifications or an unwillingness to consider parent input:

- Basing your recommendation on your schedule;
- Basing your recommendation on the school's schedule;
- Basing your recommendation on what all other students who have that particular disability category get in your district or school;
- Basing your recommendation on what an administrator told you to say;
- Telling parents the start and end dates of summer/ESY programs without individualization;
- General statements like "the way we do it here is . . ." remember the "I" in IEP!

EDUCATOR TAKEAWAY

Specifically delineating the start date, frequency, duration, and location of services AND modifications in the IEP is federally mandated. In addition, the federal regulations require that an IEP be in effect by the "beginning of the school year" for all IDEA eligible students in the local or state educational agency (20 USC 1414(d)(2)(A)). When preparing for a student's IEP Meeting, you want to strike a balance between being ready to recommend services, modifications, and a program, and not being so definitive on those recommendations that you have predetermined the child's placement without the parents' lawfully protected input.

CHAPTER 8

TRANSITION—PREPARING FOR LIFE AFTER HIGH SCHOOL

"I can't change the direction of the wind, but I can adjust my sails to always reach my destination."

—Jimmy Dean

WHAT THE LAW SAYS

The IEP must include: "Beginning not later than the first IEP to be in effect when the child is 16, or younger if determined appropriate by the IEP Team, and updated annually thereafter . . . appropriate measurable postsecondary goals based upon age appropriate transition assessments related to training, education, employment, and, where appropriate, independent living skills; the transition services (including courses of study) needed to assist the child in reaching those goals; and beginning not later than one year before the child reaches the age of majority under state law, a statement that the child has been informed of the child's rights under this chapter, if any, that will transfer to the child on reaching the age of majority."

WHAT THE LAW MEANS

Transition here is not about transition between buildings, as in when your child goes from the elementary school into middle school, or from the middle school to the high school. It is not about transitioning from class to class within a school day. This is Transition with a capital "T." It's about Transition to Adulthood! Yes, the IDEA accounts for preparing your child with a disability to be prepared for adulthood. In fact, Transition takes a front seat in the first stated purpose of the IDEA. It states

> to ensure that all children with disabilities have available to them a free appropriate public education that emphasizes special education and related services designed to meet their unique needs and *prepare them for further education, employment, and independent living.*

You will notice that this is by far the longest chapter in the book. There is a reason for this: Transition Planning is the culmination of what for many students is an entire education filled with special education services. We are hoping that the "finished product" is a student who is entering adulthood with skills and the ability to continue to avail themselves of supports where needed.

So, what the law means in this context is that school districts must begin planning for Transition to life after high school, and the planning should start early so that this planning can be as smooth and successful as possible.

Okay, so let's break this portion of the statute down.

"Beginning not later than the first IEP to be in effect when the child is 16, or younger if determined appropriate by the IEP Team, and updated annually thereafter. . . ."

This simply means that the IEP in which the child will turn sixteen must address all of the mandated elements of Transition. The law also says that the Transition portions of the IEP must be updated annually, just as all other mandated components of the IEP. In other words, the team can't consider the Transition portion of the IEP as a stagnant part of the document that gets carried over year after year.

See Commentary in the *Federal Register*, 71 Fed Reg. 46668 (August 14, 2006)

" 'Post secondary goals' . . . are generally understood to refer to those goals that a child hopes to achieve after leaving secondary school (i.e., high school)."

What is the difference between "training" and "education"? "Training" focuses on a specific area of a practical skill. Training could be shorter in duration. "Education" is broader and includes a wider range of knowledge that a student is learning. Education typically lasts for years. Think about the time it takes to go to college and other higher education pursuits.

The IEP must also include "appropriate measurable postsecondary goals based upon age appropriate transition assessments related to training, education, employment, and, where appropriate, independent living skills." Just like other goals, Transition goals are additional goals that are reconsidered every year.

The federal law also recognizes that the IEP Team can start Transition services younger than the federally mandated age of sixteen.[18]

The first step in this process is to conduct "age appropriate assessments." These assessments become the foundation on which the team builds the Transition goals. The assessments must be conducted in the specific areas of training, education, employment,

---

18 Note that under our system of government, individual states can offer more protections or services than the federal law, but not fewer. Therefore, while a state could say "we require that Transition services start younger than at 16," a state COULD NOT say "we don't start Transition Services here until age 17." Age sixteen is the maximum age at which students are entitled to have Transition Services begin.

and independent living—if, after consideration, the team believes that it is appropriate to include a student's ability to live independently.

Preparing for employment, education, and training is not optional when assessing a student's future needs; however, independent living skills are

> Many States lower the age of Transition. For example, here in Connecticut, Transition services must be in effect in the IEP when the child turns fourteen. Check with your state Department of Special Education or your school district as to when Transition services must be in place.

dependent on the individual needs of the student.

As you learned in Chapter 1 on Present Levels of Academic Achievement and Functional Performance, the goals should be based on the areas of weakness due to the student's disability that adversely impact the Transition skills the team would like the student to learn.

A student's IEP is supposed to be designed to meet their individual needs. There is no hard and fast rule about how a team determines whether it is "appropriate" to consider "independent living skills."

For example, a student with a learning disability may not lack the ability to live independently. But, considering the severity of some students' learning disabilities, the disability might impact the ability to live independently. These are the conversations that IEP Teams have to have.

Or, a student who has a neurological developmental disability like an autism spectrum disorder will more likely require skills to increase their ability to live independently. On the other hand, they may not.

Many students who have an emotional disability are also very capable intellectually and academically, so it might be the IEP Team's conclusion that a student like this won't need to be assessed or have goals created for independent living. Please don't make this assumption, as some students who profile with emotional disabilities may struggle with life skills like problem solving, initiating and planning activities, emotional regulation, and other skills needed to live independently.

Now, let's focus on this portion of the IEP Transition requirements: the IEP must include "the transition services (including courses of study) needed to assist the child in reaching those goals."

This change to the IDEA was made in the 2004 Reauthorization of the statute by Congress, and that was the first time it was made clear that preparation for post-secondary education is a requirement for those students with disabilities for whom higher education is the expected outcome after high school.

> Independent living skills are generally understood to be the skills we need in order to live on our own without any support. Depending on the severity of a student's disability, complete independence might not be the expectation, but the goal is to certainly increase independence as much as possible.
>
> Caution: Don't let it be the team's foregone conclusion that your child doesn't need to be assessed or have goals created for independent living. Nowhere in the IDEA does it say that independent living skills are reserved for those students with more severe disabilities.

Why is that so important?

Because for many, many years, Transition services were thought to be reserved for only the most profoundly intellectually or developmentally delayed students. In fact, many school teams STILL believe that they don't need to conduct Transition Assessments, develop Transition Goals, and provide Transition Services to all students with IEPs. But they do.

Therefore, if a college-bound high school student requires advanced courses of study in order to be prepared to transition to a college or university, then they are entitled to take those classes and to receive the IEP services and modifications necessary to do so successfully.

The Transition requirements go on to state that the IEP have ". . . a statement that the child has been informed of the child's rights under this chapter, if any, that will transfer to the child on reaching the age of majority."

The age (or chronological moment) at which a minor "child" legally becomes an adult is termed the "age of majority." This is the onset of adulthood. In most states, the age of majority is eighteen. When a minor child reaches the age of majority, they are considered an "adult" and become fully responsible for the obligations that society places on them. When a minor child becomes an adult, the IEP is legally under their purview and parents' legal responsibility ends.

> See Commentary in the Federal Register, page 46668: Courses of study can be "participation in advanced placement courses or a vocational education program."

> ALL students with IEPs are required to receive Transition Services, regardless of which "label" the child qualifies under.

WHAT PARENTS NEED TO KNOW

Since Transition is the culmination of all of those years of your child's, your, and the various educators' hard work, there is *a lot* to know about this final chapter of IEP mandated requirements.

Transition Services Are for *ALL* students with IEPs

First and foremost, you should know that Transition Services are for *all* students who have IEPs. It does not matter which disability your child has or how well they are doing in school. If they continue to qualify for an IEP, then by age sixteen at the latest, their IEP must address Transition.

The IDEA Rights Which You Hold on Your Child's Behalf Transfer to Them After Age Eighteen[19]

Next, you need to know that once your child reaches the age of majority, which in most States is age eighteen, all of their rights under the IDEA "transfer" from you to them. *Once that*

---

19 Some States set the Age of Majority at an older age than eighteen.

happens, you no longer have the legal authority to make educational decisions for your child. This is one of the reasons that the IDEA requires that Students be informed by their school districts one year prior to reaching the age of majority that this will happen in a year. The intent is to give the student and the family time to discuss and plan based on that student's needs and preferences.

There are ways that you can continue to have educational decision-making authority alongside your child when they reach the age of majority. For legally competent individuals who want their parents to continue to make educational decisions for them, they can execute an Educational Power of Attorney, which is a signed legal document that authorizes a person's parents (or any other designee they choose) to act on their behalf.

In addition, for students that are not able to execute a Power of Attorney because they lack legal competence, there are other ways that parents and other adults in a young person's life can obtain decision-making authority, through guardianships, conservatorships, and similar types of models.

A note here, however: The whole point of the IDEA is to create independent adults, and your now-adult child, in most cases, should be able to make their own decisions. As with all other areas related to disability, we presume competence first.

Transition Services Can Extend to Twenty-One (minimally)

Transition services can extend minimally to the age of twenty-one. Yes, beyond your child's traditional senior year in high school.

Your Child's Transition Services End If They Are "Exited" Prior to Aging Out

In addition to "aging out" of services, your child can be exited from special education when your child is evaluated and determined to no longer be a child with a disability. Yes, this can certainly happen. For example, if your child has a learning disability and the special education and related services they received were so impactful, when your child is evaluated, the testing shows that no area of disability remains. It is then determined they are participating and making progress in the general education curriculum and no longer eligible for special education. In this case, the Transition Services would also terminate.

> Transition Services Can Extend to Twenty-One
>
> 20 USC 1412(a)(1)(A)
>
> Free Appropriate Public Education
>
> "A free appropriate public education is available to all children with disabilities residing in the state between the ages of 3 and 21, inclusive, including children with disabilities who have been suspended or expelled from school."
>
> Check the cut-off age that a student can receive Transition services in your state, as many states have ages that exceed twenty-one years of age. In your state, your child may be able to receive services for another year or several beyond age twenty-one.

However, the federal regulations do not allow this to happen unless your child was evaluated to determine that they are no longer eligible:

You should know about person-centered planning

Person-Centered Planning can yield a great deal of insight into your child's future after high school and can be considered a fruitful way to kick-off the Transition planning process.

Person-centered planning is a process, not an assessment, conducted by someone who has been trained in the process. Participants include the school team, the student and their family, friends, and other stakeholders who come together to focus on the student's vision for the future. Other people who are invested in the student are involved in the process to also share their insight and thoughts about the student.

---

34 CFR Sec. 300.305 Additional requirements for evaluations and reevaluations
Evaluations before change in eligibility
(1) ". . . a public agency must evaluate a child with a disability . . . before determining that the child is no longer a child with a disability.

Sec. 300.305 Additional requirements for evaluations and reevaluations
(2) ". . . An evaluation (to determine if the child has a disability) is not required before the termination of a child's eligibility.... due to graduation from secondary school with a regular diploma, or due to exceeding the age eligibility for FAPE under state law.
(3) For a child whose eligibility terminates .....a public agency must provide the child with a summary of the child's academic achievement and functional performance, which shall include recommendations on how to assist the child in meeting the child's postsecondary goals.

This process is a great way to identify what your child wants versus what the school district traditionally offers. This process can be modified to fit the individual needs of the student and is designed to identify goals and dreams, avoid unwanted outcomes, and pin down the people and resources to help realize their goals for the future.

There is no specific time to conduct this process. We have seen it done in middle school and then again in high school. It is ideal to do in the beginning stages of Transition or early high school which can be used to further add to the PLAAFP and enhance the Transition planning process.

You can ask the school team to conduct a person-centered planning. There are several programs available, such as (PATH) (Pearpoint, O'Brien, & Forest, 1991), and McGill Action Planning System (MAPS) (Vandercook & York, 1989).

You Have a Right to Refuse Your Child's High School Diploma

When your child receives a high school diploma, they are terminated from special education services. This means they forfeit their right to continue to receive special education from their school district. However, in most States you would have to take action in the form of filing for a Due Process Hearing to stop the diploma.

For some students, the mere fact that they have earned enough credits to receive a diploma does NOT mean they have made enough progress towards their Transition goals that they are ready to graduate. You, or your child if they are over the age of majority, can notify the district that you do not agree with the issuance of the diploma.

> Graduation is a "change in placement" which means you have the right under "stay put" protections to file for a Hearing and ask that your child not be issued the diploma. **But you must take action before the diploma is issued,** so don't wait until the week or two before graduation to weigh in on this with your IEP Team.

Your school team might determine and recommend that your child no longer requires special education and exit them from special education before you think they are ready. Or, they may say that since your child has earned enough credits to graduate, they should receive their diploma.

In these situations, you can attempt to convince the school team otherwise. However, if the team disagrees and exits your child while you disagree, you have no other choice but to file for a Due Process Hearing to invoke your Stay Put rights. This may require you retaining counsel. When you file for Due Process, your child's special education services are "frozen" and stay in place until it is determined through a hearing, settlement agreement, or litigation that your child is exited from or continues their special education.

However, refusing the diploma does not mean your child should be deprived of Senior Year activities and celebrations!

What will the diploma look like? In our experience, many students with disabilities are resistant to go on with special education after their traditional senior year for fear their friends and other students will learn that they will not receive their official diploma. Many students, rightly so, are concerned that other students will know their "diploma" will look different. They should not be singled out in any way that makes it obvious that their "diploma" is different.

Students who are still working out how to disclose their disability should have the right and dignity to keep their diploma status private. Ask what it will look like so you can rest assured your child will not stand out as having a different "diploma." Ask for the font type and lettering size to be the same so it will look

---

Section 1415 (j)

(j) Maintenance of current educational placement

(k)(4) ". . . . during the pendency of any proceedings conducted . . . ., unless the state or local educational agency and the parents otherwise agree, the child shall remain in the then-current educational placement of the child, or, if applying for initial admission to a public school, shall, with the consent of the parents, be placed in the public school program until all such proceedings have been completed."

Even if you reject the diploma, a special education student can "walk" with their class and go through all of the graduation ceremonies and festivities and take a non-diploma or certificate-of-attendance and continue their status as a special education student with an IEP.

similar to the regular diploma and that the holder or cover is the same as others receiving their diplomas.

When Will Students Continuing Special Education Receive Their Official Diploma?

Students extending their high school special education after their customary senior year will receive their diploma upon exiting from special education or upon aging out of special education because they have exceeded the age of eligibility in their state.

Exiting from special education can happen at any time the IEP team determines the student has met all of their goals and it is determined that services are no longer needed, and has been re-evaluated and no longer meets the criteria of a student with a disability, or the parent or student (who has reached the age of majority) requests that services be terminated.

When your child is exited from special education, they will receive their regular diploma the year in which they have technically graduated and take their official diploma. Students cannot have the diploma reflect the year of their customary senior year.

Students Don't Require Their Diploma to Take College Classes

Some students who continue to receive special education services beyond their traditional senior year might take a college course or two as part of their movement toward preparing for college as part of their Transition programming. We've had parents share their concern that if their child doesn't get their diploma, they can't enroll in any college classes. This is simply not the case.

Colleges need to know if your child has completed all of their high school credits, which is reflected in their high school transcript. As long as your child has completed their credits for the classes they have completed in high school, the only thing they should need to produce for the college is their high school transcript of credits.

Should the college require your child's diploma, you or your child should go to the college's disability office and explain that they are a special education student who is participating in Transition services. Should they refuse and continue to insist that your child must produce their diploma, you can provide your child's "non-diploma" and request a reasonable accommodation under the ADA to not produce their diploma.

> 34 CFR. 300.102 (a)
>
> (a) General. The obligation to make FAPE available to all children with disabilities does not apply with respect to the following:
>
> (3)
> (i) Children with disabilities who have graduated from high school with a regular high school diploma.

Services Don't Have to Take Place at the High School After Your Child's Traditional Senior Year

Your school district might have their Transition services housed at the high school or in another school building within the district.

This is not necessarily inappropriate for all students, but we want you to know that Transition services must be individualized, and it might not be an appropriate placement decision for all students.

If your child is going to receive Transition services beyond the typical senior year, there's a legal argument to be made that services should not take place at their high school or other schools in the district with younger children. Why?

It's a matter of dignity and a person's right to be free from disability-based discrimination. We wouldn't expect nondisabled high school graduates to continue their education either by remaining at their high school, or suddenly being educated in a building with much younger peers, so we shouldn't expect it for our disabled students. As we have said to many administrators when they suggest the student who is a high school senior but needs ongoing services just "stay another two years here at the high school," would YOU want to have stayed at your high school another two years after your classmates all graduated?

We should not be holding our students with disabilities to a different standard than their peers without disabilities.

Heck, we know of situations where Transition programs are housed in the building where students went to grade school and they are located next to a classroom of preschoolers. We've seen the negative impact this has had on students. Remember, we should be expecting the same dignity experienced by non-disabled students who are going on to college, vocational programs, technical schools, internships, or employment.

> When You Disagree with "Where" Transition Services Take Place After the Traditional 12th Year:
>
> You have the right to disagree and exercise your due process rights.
>
> Your school district will most likely offer Transition programming that is a part of their district's programming. They have a legal obligation to provide you with a continuum of services that will be most appropriate for your child.
>
> You should explore all options and work with the school district to understand the continuum of services within the district and outside of the district.

If your IEP team determines that your school district's Transition programming is appropriate for your child, find out where their non-community programming takes place. If it is in a district school, speak up and ask for the location to be changed if you don't believe it is appropriate for your child.

Be Ahead of Transition Before It's Upon You; Don't Let It Be an Afterthought

We can't tell you how many parents come to us when their child is in their senior year of high school and are just learning of "Transition" services and that their child has the option to continue their special education services. Unfortunately, far too many times, we see that the legally mandated aspects of Transition are minimally accounted for on the IEP paperwork, and it is not reviewed with the parents during their IEP team meetings. We're not saying that every school district underestimates Transition services, but we've seen it enough to alert you to the fact that once your child is reaching Transition age in your state, please be ever mindful of going through the legally mandated processes in the statute we have included here.

Talk with your team about Transition before it legally has to take place. Ask them to explain the process to you.

Finally, some areas of need include subjects that parents and school teams may find difficult to discuss, like relationship safety, sexual knowledge, mental health, dangerous behaviors, internet safety, or other areas that can be embarrassing to discuss. Remember, this is your child's future at stake here. If there is a concerning barrier to functioning in the world beyond high school, don't hesitate to raise it as an area to be assessed in accordance with your child's unique needs. If the school team does not have an assessment for the area of concern, you and your school team can reach out to your state's Department of Special Education to determine what other resources your state might have to identify and use assessments.

PARENT TAKEAWAY

We like to say that you can't know how to get there if you don't know where you are going. In other words, successful planning for Transition to adulthood is best accomplished by identifying your target and creating a map on how to get there.

We know that Transition is an awful lot to take in. There are many moving parts and it can be overwhelming. Start thinking about what your child's needs will be for employment, post-secondary education, and independent living as early as possible so you can work with your team to be realistic about the planning and implementation process.

Ask your school district and/or state Department of Special Education to provide you with resources that your state utilizes for Transition Services. Start asking about the Transition process as early as you can so you are not trying to execute a last-minute plan in the eleventh hour.

WHAT EDUCATORS AND RELATED PROFESSIONALS NEED TO KNOW

Transition services are not reserved for certain types of students with disabilities; they are REQUIRED to be provided by age sixteen or sooner for all students who have IEPs. In addition, they must be individualized just like all other aspects of the IEP.

Have you ever had to explain to a parent that the school team can't address a parent's concern in the IEP because the concern in question is not seen or displayed at school? This might be an appropriate explanation. After all, a lagging skill resulting from a child's disability must affect "the child's involvement and progress in the general education curriculum."

This is part of the definition of an IEP (Sec. 300.320 Definition of individualized education program), which also goes on to say to also "meet each of the child's other educational needs that result from the child's disability . . ."

It's clear to us that goals need to allow a student to be "involved in and make progress" in the general education curriculum but they can also "meet other needs that result from the child's disability," *before* they become Transition age.

While that understanding of the statute might create a legal disagreement among teams and parents, there is no doubt that once a student becomes Transition age, that Transition goals should be developed considering the student's movement toward post-school life in the real world of employment, post-secondary education and, if appropriate, independent living. All of these things include functioning outside of the school walls. These post-school activities take place at home and in the community.

We understand that Transition might seem like a part of the IEP in which your involvement might not be needed. You might think that Transition is left up to the person or people on the school team who traditionally contribute to Transition.

> Your students are not going to be living the rest of their lives at school. . . . Are they ready for it? What do you need to do to get them ready?

However, if comprehensive assessments are done in post-secondary training and education, employment and, if appropriate, independent living, this information can reveal skills that likely require further supports and services from speech and language pathologists, OTs, PTs, reading specialists, counselors, etc.

For example, let's say an assessment, or input from a student or parent, reveals that a student wants to input data on a computer as part of their employment, but the student does not know how to type. The team could determine that the OT, a related service, needs to be added into the IEP to teach this skill.

Engage parents in the process of discussing Transition. Your school district has a legal obligation under the IDEA to inform parents of when the Transition process starts and when students reach the age of majority and their educational decision-making rights over the IEP transfer to them. You can go above and beyond these mandates and involve parents as early as you believe a discussion about Transition should begin. Involve parents every step of the way.

Engage students in the Transition Process. Your school district probably has practices on when and how you engage students in their Transition planning. Check with your district, your state's Parent Information Center, or state Department of Special Education for resources on Transition and engaging students.

However, please remember that Transition services can begin before the age of sixteen (or the age determined in your state). If you believe that a student's Transition services should start earlier, speak up.

Too frequently, we see IEP Teams getting to the very end of the Annual Review right before the student turns sixteen and simply "checking off" the Transition part of the form without much discussion or thought. This is a big mistake, and for a number of reasons.

> Get in the habit of checking dates of birth when you are preparing to attend a child's IEP Meeting, so that if this is the last IEP meeting prior to the student turning sixteen, you are prepared to discuss Transition Assessments, goals and services.

The path forward for many students with disabilities may require more planning than the average student who does not have disabilities. Depending on what the student in question's adult life is expected to entail, you may need an entirely separate meeting to discuss Transition.

One big mistake we see here is with the first step: assessments. Many times we learn that the information the IEP is relying on to develop Transition Goals are the very same post-secondary interest inventories and instruments that the high school administers to ALL students in their junior year. That is not individualization and will form an improper foundation for designing an individualized Transition Program.

Further, just asking the parents or student at the end of the meeting what the child "wants to be when they grow up" is a start, but not an end, of the conversation. What if the answer is "Superman"? We should be utilizing reliable testing instruments to assess where a student's skills are relative to employment, independent living, and post-secondary education preparation.

> The Transition Planning Inventory (TPI)
>
> As a starting point, consider asking your school district to conduct The Transition Planning Inventory (TPI). This particular assessment tool addresses the critical Transition planning areas that are mandated by the 2004 IDEA.

You can break the "that's how we do it here" mold! We experience school teams telling parents, "We don't work on employment until their senior year," or "We don't do more comprehensive assessments until their junior year." We understand that schools put practices in place that help implement Transition services to make the process manageable for their school teams. This typically results in carrying out set Transition steps in middle school and a student's freshman, sophomore, junior, and senior years respectfully. We see the point in having an order to Transition planning, but please remember that Transition must be an individualized process.

Please, please be ahead of the game with Transition. Some school districts have Transition "specialists" or personnel who are responsible for supporting the team in Transition planning. If you believe you need the support of a specialist like this, let your school arrange this for you.

The Transfer of Rights, likewise, is not something we want overlooked. In most states, the discussion with the student that their rights under the IDEA will transfer to them must begin by the student's seventeenth birthday. The purpose of giving a full year of notice to the student is so that they, and their family, can begin planning for how and whether the student will make their educational decisions. If you don't believe a student with whom you are working is likely to be legally competent, you want to point the family to community resources as soon as possible so they can obtain decision-making authority for their child. This requires planning, and ensuring that you have fulfilled the obligation to inform on the Transfer of rights at least a full year prior to the student reaching the age of majority is crucial.

The IDEA and its implementing regulations define Transition Services broadly:

34 CFR Sec. 300.43 Transition services

If your school's IEP software programs or systems allow it, find a way to set a "teaser" so that you are reminded that the student is reaching one year prior to the age of majority. If the system doesn't have that feature, come up with an internal way of making sure you aren't missing this deadline.

(a) Transition services means a coordinated set of activities for a child with a disability that—

1. Is designed to be within a results-oriented process, that is focused on improving the academic and functional achievement of the child with a disability to facilitate the child's movement from school to post-school activities, including postsecondary education, vocational education, integrated employment (including supported employment), continuing and adult education, adult services, independent living, or community participation;

2. Is based on the individual child's needs, taking into account the child's strengths, preferences, and interests; and includes—
   (i) Instruction;
   (ii) Related services;
   (iii) Community experiences;
   (iv) The development of employment and other post-school adult living objectives; and
   (v) If appropriate, acquisition of daily living skills and provision of a functional vocational evaluation.

(b) Transition services for children with disabilities may be special education, if provided as specially designed instruction, or a related service, if required to assist a child with a disability to benefit from special education.

Individual States can both lower the minimum age that Transition must be considered (e.g., starting at age fourteen rather than sixteen) and raise the maximum age for eligibility (e.g., through age twenty-three instead of twenty-one). However, they can't do the opposite; in other words, the federal law requires a window from age sixteen through twenty-one for students who don't get a diploma sooner, and a state can't say that window is shorter, but they can offer more time as part of Transition Services.

34 CFR Sec. 300.305 Additional requirements for evaluations and reevaluations
Evaluations before change in eligibility
(1) ". . . a public agency must evaluate a child with a disability . . . before determining that the child is no longer a child with a disability.

34 CFR Sec. 300.305 Additional requirements for evaluations and reevaluations
(2) ". . . An evaluation (to determine if the child has a disability) is not required before the termination of a child's eligibility. . . . due to graduation from secondary school with a regular diploma, or due to exceeding the age eligibility for FAPE under state law.
(3) For a child whose eligibility terminates .....a public agency must provide the child with a summary of the child's academic achievement and functional performance, which shall include recommendations on how to assist the child in meeting the child's postsecondary goals.

As an educator, you may believe that a student no longer qualifies for special education even though they are Transition Age. That is fine, provided you follow all of the procedures for terminating services. Essential to that is to have recently conducted testing that demonstrates that the student is no longer eligible under the IDEA.

If you are recommending that a student is ready for their diploma, but the student or parents disagree, you should be aware that they have the right to file for a Due Process Hearing to stop the issuance of the diploma. Federal law says that graduation from high school is a "change in placement" just like any other change in placement under the IDEA. When there is a disagreement over whether graduation is appropriate, parents and students have the right to be informed that they have procedural safeguards that allow them to challenge the IEP Team's decision.

Once it is determined that a student will, in fact, be completing their IDEA entitlements, the IDEA requires that a Summary of Performance be completed. The Summary of Performance (SOP) is a summary of academic achievement and functional performance. The purpose of the SOP is to lay out critical information for people who might be helping the student with postsecondary goals and ambitions.

> 34 CFR Sec. 300.102 (a)
> FAPE Requirements
> (iii) Graduation from high school with a regular high school diploma constitutes a change in placement, requiring written prior notice.

The SOP must be finalized in the last year of your child's high school education and should include the student's participation in the process. It is not a requirement that it be developed at an IEP Team Meeting. Further, the IDEA does not specify what must be included in the SOP. Check with your state's Department of Special Education to see if specific information must be included in accordance with your state's guidelines or policy.

Don't forget to consider independent living. We routinely experience school teams who have come to the conclusion that students without intellectual disability do not require Transition goals for independent living before their traditional twelfth grade year or after. Please remember that the IDEA does not say a student has to have an intellectual disability to be eligible for independent living goals.

Don't Underestimate the Myriad of Skills Required for Independent Living

The IDEA requires that the IEP must have goals for independent living, if appropriate. There are plenty of scenarios where goals for children with disabilities we don't typically consider needing independent living goals are appropriate. For example, take a student whose disability involves their mental health (depression, anxiety, etc.) and how that might impact their ability to manage all of the skills they will need to meet the demands of everyday life. This can include their health and safety, self-care, leisure skills, social skills, self-direction, and participation in the community, as examples.

We simply ask that you take the time to think through independent living goals for all of your students. You could be surprised how their disability just might need independent living goals. Think beyond their academic abilities and consider health and safety, community use, home or school living, self-care, leisure skills, social skills, self-direction, functional academics, communication, etc.

Let's discuss the college-bound student with an IEP. Part of that student's IDEA entitlements is to be prepared, through their IEP, for post-secondary education. This has many implications and includes that the student be given access to advanced placement and honors courses with the supports necessary to be successful in them.

When considering the IEP for college-bound students, we also need to spend some time discussing modifications.

Modifications

We come across too many students who have been slated to receive diplomas whose IEPs still reflect modifications.

Remember, college students and other post-secondary educational institutions are not required to provide students modifications. Given this, it's important to plan for fading modifications, if possible. If a student will always require modifications, then this is an important discussion to have with parents to drive the decision of realistic post-secondary education options.

Modifications vs. Accommodations.

Modifications change "what" is taught or expected from the student, thus making assignments easier and reducing the expectations. Examples include less homework, alternate projects, assignments, books, and grading. Students are not expected to meet the same demands as other students.

An accommodation is typically an environmental or physical alteration that helps the student work around their disability. Students are expected to meet the same demands as other students, but their accommodations made it easier for them to access the task or demand. Accommodation examples include extra time for assignments and tests, preferential seating, pencil grips, sign language interpretation, and oral test taking, to name just a few.

Modifications and accommodations are based on the unique needs of each student with a disability.

College Programs for Students With Intellectual Disabilities:

Comprehensive Transition Programs, or CTPs, are programs that offer degrees, certificates, or non-degrees for students who have intellectual disabilities and who meet specific criteria. Check CTP programs in your state.

Accommodations

Reasonable accommodations are allowed in college and other post-secondary educational institutions under the ADA. This is also true for places of employment. Students should be taught to go to their college's disability office or human resources at their place of employment to disclose their disability and apply for accommodations.

One of the most important aspects of Transition Planning is preparing your students to become their own self-advocates. Yes, self-advocacy skills are important for all individuals, but once Transition Aged, this is essential. The federal laws which protect individuals in our primary and secondary schools are obligations to be followed by the school teams. Once the student leaves that system, it is incumbent on them to ask for accommodations. And in order to receive accommodations in college or in a place of employment, individuals with disabilities must disclose their disability and provide proof of their disability. At college, this takes place at the disability office, and in a place of work, this takes place with human resources. However, some students may not wish to disclose their disability. If students determine they would rather not disclose their disability, it's essential to make sure their goals are geared to master the skills they will need if not provided with the accommodation.

Students cannot begin to know how to ask for accommodations if the first time they are even aware of their status as a person with a disability is when they graduate from high school!

We suggest incorporating goals and services into the IEP well before then, which will enable the student to start to understand their disability, how it impacts them, and the best way for them to avail themselves of resources in the community to help them receive any accommodations to which they may be entitled in further education, employment, housing, etc.

> **Accommodations Under the ADA**
>
> Under the ADA, a federal disability law, students with disabilities can receive reasonable accommodations. However, in order to receive accommodations, students must disclose their disability to apply for accommodations. It's important to teach students how to apply for accommodations and to know what accommodations they will need in a post-secondary education setting.
>
> If a student has accommodations under an IEP or a 504 plan, the accommodations transfer to college under the ADA.

EDUCATOR TAKEAWAY

Just as it is for parents, we know that Transition to adulthood can be an overwhelming process for educators. Your role in Transition planning for students might be limited or you may be taking a front seat. Regardless, partner with parents and start this process as early as possible. The outcomes will be so much better with proper assessment, planning, and services.

PART THREE
RESOURCES

COMMON SPECIAL EDUCATION TERMINOLOGY

The following is by no means a complete list of all terms you may encounter in the field of special education, and new terms, tests and methodologies develop every day, along with diagnoses of various disabilities. We hope this is a good start, though!

Academic Achievement
Academic Achievement is a measure of the progress made toward acquiring academic skills and knowledge that are taught in school and include learning in areas like math, reading, writing, etc.

Accommodation
Accommodations are provided to students with disabilities to enable them to access the general education curriculum. What they are learning, producing, and how they are graded are the same expectations as nondisabled students. Unlike a modification, which is a change to what the student is taught, expected to learn, and possibly graded. (see modification)

Annual Goal
An annual goal is a learning target developed for one school year
by the IEP team that describes an academic or functional (non-
academic) skill (see functional skills) that a student can achieve in
one school year.

AR (Annual Review)
This is the time when a child's IEP must be reviewed at least once
a year. Typically, the AR date is dictated by the date the student
was deemed eligible for an IEP.

ABA (Applied Behavior Analysis)
A widely accepted definition of Applied Behavior Analysis is
"the process of systematically applying interventions based upon
the principles of learning theory to improve socially significant
behaviors to a meaningful degree, and to demonstrate that the
interventions employed are responsible for the improvement in
behavior."[20]

APE (Adaptive Physical Education)
An alternative physical education program for students with disabilities who may not be able to successfully participate in regular
physical education. APE is individualized for the unique capabilities and needs of each student.

Assessment
A systematic method of gathering information from tests and
other sources to determine whether a child is a child with a disability and to determine the special educational needs of the child.

AT (Assistive Technology)
Assistive technology (AT) is any item, piece of equipment,
software program, or product system that is used to increase,

---

20 Baer, Wolf & Risley, 1968; Sulzer-Azaroff & Mayer, 1991

maintain, or improve the functional capabilities of persons with disabilities.

BCBA (Board Certified Behavior Analyst)
A Board Certified Behavior Analyst is a graduate-level certification in behavior analysis. BCBAs provide behavior-analytic services.

BIP (Behavior Intervention Plan)
A Behavior Intervention Plan addresses behaviors that interfere with a students' learning or that of others; based on data gathered through a Functional Behavioral Assessment. The Plan specifies the actions to take to improve or replace the target behavior(s) identified in an FBA.

Child with a Disability[21]
A child with a disability means a child evaluated as having an intellectual disability, a hearing impairment (including deafness), a speech or language impairment, a visual impairment (including blindness), a serious emotional disturbance (referred to in this part as "emotional disturbance"),[22] an orthopedic impairment, autism, traumatic brain injury, another health impairment, a specific learning disability, deaf-blindness, or multiple disabilities, and who, by reason thereof, needs special education and related services.

The following thirteen disability categories are defined in Sec. 300.8 of the IDEA:

---

21 While the IDEA spells out thirteen eligibility categories, individual States can, and do, offer additional categories, for example a specific ADHD label instead of just falling under OHI.

22 The term "Emotional Disturbance" is incredibly outdated and in our view, an antiquated viewpoint about individuals with mental health challenges. In Connecticut, we banded together to get our state to change the label to "Emotional Disability," and encourage others to do the same in their States until hopefully it is changed by Congress.

Autism

Autism means a developmental disability significantly affecting verbal and nonverbal communication and social interaction, generally evident before age three, that adversely affects a child's educational performance. Other characteristics often associated with autism are engagement in repetitive activities and stereotyped movements, resistance to environmental change or change in daily routines, and unusual responses to sensory experiences.

Deaf-blindness

Deaf-blindness means concomitant hearing and visual impairments, the combination of which causes such severe communication and other developmental and educational needs that they cannot be accommodated in special education programs solely for children with deafness or children with blindness.

Deafness

Deafness means a hearing impairment that is so severe that the child is impaired in processing linguistic information through hearing, with or without amplification, that adversely affects a child's educational performance.

Emotional Disturbance (ED)

ED means a condition exhibiting one or more of the following characteristics over a long period of time and to a marked degree that adversely affects a child's educational performance:

an inability to learn that cannot be explained by intellectual, sensory, or health factors; an inability to build or maintain satisfactory interpersonal relationships with peers and teachers; inappropriate types of behavior or feelings under normal circumstances; a general pervasive mood of unhappiness or depression; a tendency to develop physical symptoms or fears associated with personal or school problems. Emotional disturbance includes schizophrenia. The term does not apply to children who are socially maladjusted, unless it is determined that they have an emotional disturbance.

Hearing Impairment

Hearing impairment means an impairment in hearing, whether permanent or fluctuating, that adversely affects a child's educational performance but that is not included under the definition of deafness.

Intellectual Disability (ID)

Intellectual disability means significantly subaverage general intellectual functioning, existing concurrently with deficits in adaptive behavior, and manifested during the developmental period, that adversely affects a child's educational performance. The term "intellectual disability" was formerly termed "mental retardation."

Multiple Disabilities

Multiple disabilities means concomitant impairments (such as intellectual disability-blindness or intellectual disability-orthopedic impairment), the combination of which causes such severe educational needs that they cannot be accommodated in special education programs solely for one of the impairments. Multiple disabilities does not include deaf-blindness.

Orthopedic Impairment

Orthopedic impairment means a severe orthopedic impairment that adversely affects a child's educational performance. The term includes impairments caused by a congenital anomaly, impairments caused by disease (e.g., poliomyelitis, bone tuberculosis), and impairments from other causes (e.g., cerebral palsy, amputations, and fractures or burns that cause contractures).

Other Health Impairment (OHI)

Other health impairment means having limited strength, vitality, or alertness, including a heightened alertness to environmental stimuli, that results in limited alertness with respect to the educational environment, that is due to chronic or acute health problems such as asthma, attention deficit disorder or attention deficit hyperactivity disorder, diabetes, epilepsy, a heart condition, hemophilia, lead poisoning, leukemia, nephritis, rheumatic fever, sickle cell anemia, and Tourette syndrome; and adversely affects a child's educational performance.

Specific Learning Disability (LD or SLD)

A specific learning disability means a disorder in one or more of the basic psychological processes involved in understanding or in using language, spoken or written, that may manifest itself in the imperfect ability to listen, think, speak, read, write, spell, or to do mathematical calculations, including conditions such as perceptual disabilities, brain injury, minimal brain dysfunction, dyslexia, and developmental aphasia.

Specific learning disability does not include learning problems that are primarily the result of visual, hearing, or motor disabilities, of intellectual disability, of emotional disturbance, or of environmental, cultural, or economic disadvantage.

Speech or Language Impairment

A speech or language impairment means a communication disorder, such as stuttering, impaired articulation, a language impairment, or a voice impairment, that adversely affects a child's educational performance.

Traumatic Brain Injury

A traumatic brain injury means an acquired injury to the brain caused by an external physical force, resulting in total or partial functional disability or psychosocial impairment, or both, that adversely affects a child's educational performance. Traumatic brain injury applies to open or closed head injuries resulting in impairments in one or more areas, such as cognition; language; memory; attention; reasoning; abstract thinking; judgment; problem-solving; sensory, perceptual, and motor abilities; psychosocial behavior; physical functions; information processing; and speech. Traumatic brain injury does not apply to brain injuries that are congenital or degenerative, or to brain injuries induced by birth trauma.

Visual Impairment

A visual impairment including blindness means an impairment in vision that, even with correction, adversely affects a child's educational performance. The term includes both partial sight and blindness.

Developmental Delay

Not one of the thirteen categories of disability, a developmental delay can be a disability classification given to a child aged three through nine (or any subset of that age range, including ages three through five), who is experiencing developmental delays, as defined by the state and as measured by appropriate diagnostic instruments and procedures, in one or more of the following areas: Physical development, cognitive development, communication development, social or emotional development, or adaptive development; and who, by reason thereof, needs special education and related services.

Diploma

A certificate earned by students who graduate from high school by meeting graduation requirements set by the state in which the student resides.

Certification of Attendance

A certificate of attendance is typically provided to students with disabilities who "age out" or graduate from high school but who have not met the state mandated graduation requirements. Certificates of Attendance do not certify specific knowledge or skills, only attendance. Some States have their own "diploma" and/or "certificate" options for students with disabilities.

Common Core Standards
National standards developed to conform the kindergarten to twelfth grade learning expectations of students throughout the United States. The common core can serve as a target range of skills to measure the learning gap between regular education students and special education students.

Compensatory Education
Compensatory Education refers to make-up services or education awarded to or agreed upon for a child when the school district violates the IEP or fails to provide services or education.

Consent
A requirement that a parent is fully informed in writing regarding that action that a school district is proposing to take about a child.

Core Academic Subjects
Core academic subjects generally include English; civics and government; reading or language arts; economics; mathematics; arts; science; history; geography and foreign languages.

Curriculum
An instructional program or course of study that is arranged into a scope (the areas of learning that the curriculum will cover) and sequence (the order in which the skills are taught).

ESY (Extended School Year)
A school district is required to provide ESY services, or services over the summer months, when a special education student's team determines, on an individual basis, that the child requires ESY to receive a free and appropriate public education. ESY cannot be limited to particular categories of disability or limit the type, amount, or duration of the services.

Extended School Day
A lengthened school day for a special education student to receive instruction beyond the standard school day.

FAPE (Free Appropriate Public Education)
FAPE is a cornerstone of the IDEA. Students with disabilities are entitled to their public education just as students without disabilities. In order to receive and benefit from that education, students with disabilities may require special education and related services. Their education needs to be

Free—at no cost to the parent;

Appropriate—provided an IEP that outlines a program to meet their unique needs that is "reasonably calculated to enable a child to make progress appropriate in light of the child's circumstances"; [23]

Public—the same public schools that children without disabilities attend; and

Education—the courses and educational opportunities offered by a school district.

FBA (Functional Behavior Assessment)
A Functional Behavioral Assessment is a process that identifies a target behavior(s) that interferes with a student's education. The assessment identifies what is maintaining or causing a challenging behavior. The process leads to a Behavior Intervention Plan (BIP) or intervention plan to help the student develop more appropriate alternate behaviors.

FERPA (Family Education Rights and Privacy Act)
FERPA is a federal law that allows parents the right to have access to their children's education records, the right to seek to

---

23 "Appropriate" as defined by the *Endrew F.* Supreme Court decision in 2017.

have the records amended, and the right to have some control over the disclosure of personally identifiable information from the education records.

FOIA (Freedom of Information Act)
FOIA provides that any person has the right to request access to federal agency records.

Functional Performance
A measure of a student's skills that are not academic, but rather comprise skills for everyday competencies that help individuals meet the demands of one's environment, including the skills necessary to effectively and independently take care of oneself and to interact with other people.

IDEA (Individuals with Disabilities Education Act)
The Individuals with Disabilities Education Act is the federal law that supports special education and related service programming for children with disabilities.

IEE (Independent Educational Evaluation)
Parents of a child with a disability have a right to disagree with a district's evaluation(s) and request an IEE, an evaluation conducted by a qualified evaluator who is not employed by the school district. (see chapter on Procedural Safeguards)

IEP (Individualized Education Program)
An IEP is a written statement, or the document developed, that describes the educational program designed to meet a child's individual needs.

IEP Team
In accordance with Sec. 300.321, ". . . The required members of the Individualized Education Program Team must include the parents of the child; not less than one regular education teacher of the child (if the child is, or may be, participating in the

regular education environment); not less than one special education teacher of the child, or where appropriate, not less than one
special education provider of the child; a representative of the
public agency who is qualified to provide, or supervise the provision of, specially designed instruction to meet the unique needs
of children with disabilities; is knowledgeable about the general
education curriculum; and is knowledgeable about the availability
of resources of the public agency.

An individual who can interpret the instructional implications
of evaluation results, who may be a member of the team; at the
discretion of the parent or the agency, other individuals who have
knowledge or special expertise regarding the child, including
related services personnel as appropriate; and whenever appropriate, the child with a disability. . . ."

Impartial Due Process Hearing
The Opportunity for a parent to file a Complaint under the
IDEA regarding the identification, evaluation, or services and
placement offered to their child, and to have the matter heard
before an Impartial Hearing Officer. See chapter on Procedural
Safeguards.

Inclusion
Sometimes referred to as "mainstreaming" is when special education students are provided full participation in the general education curriculum.

Initial Evaluation
An initial evaluation determines whether a student is eligible to
receive special education services or needs an IEP.

LEA (Local Education Agency)
The LEA is your local school district that has administrative control and direction of your public elementary school or secondary
school, including a public charter school.

LRE (Least Restrictive Environment)
Least Restrictive Environment (LRE) is a principle that guides where and how special education will be provided. The LRE provision of the IDEA provides that:

> To the maximum extent appropriate, children with disabilities, including children in public or private institutions or other care facilities, are educated with children who are not disabled, and special classes, separate schooling, or other removal of children with disabilities from the regular educational environment occurs only when the nature or severity of the disability of a child is such that education in regular classes with the use of supplementary aids and services cannot be achieved satisfactorily. (20 U.S.C. § 1412(a)(5)(A))

Manifestation Determination
An IEP meeting with the purpose of determining whether or not a behavior, which violated a school rule and resulted in suspension for ten days or more, was caused by the student's disability and/or the IEP not being implemented.

Mediation
A voluntary dispute resolution process in which an impartial mediator assists the parties in resolving issues in dispute. See the chapter on Procedural Safeguards.

Methodology
A methodology is an established educational approach that is specific and systematic that follows prescribed techniques or steps that allows repeated opportunities for students to practice a task.

Modification
Unlike an accommodation that does not change what a student is taught or expected to learn, a modification changes *what* a student is expected to learn and produce compared to their general education peers. Grading can also be adjusted to the individual needs of the student.

OCR (US Office for Civil Rights)
The federal government agency of the executive branch within the Department of Education that is charged with enforcing federal civil rights laws, including Section 504.

OG (Orton Gillingham)
A multi-sensory, scientifically researched and verified method of providing remediation to students with dyslexia and other learning disabilities.

OSEP (Office of Special Education Programs)
A division within the Office of Special Education Programs and Rehabilitation Services with duties including administering the IDEA and its mission is to improve outcomes for children with disabilities, birth through twenty-one, and their families, ensuring access to fair, equitable, and high-quality education and services.

OSERS (Office of Special Education and Rehabilitative Services)
An agency of the federal government's executive branch within the Department of Education that supports programs that help educate children and youth with disabilities and provides for the rehabilitation of youth and adults with disabilities.

Paraprofessional
An adult individual who is under the direct supervision of qualified personnel or a licensed teacher who provides direct support to a child, or to a teacher or other school professional in assisting them with the management of the classroom or other settings that are non-academic.

Parent
A biological or adoptive parent, surrogate parent with educational decision making rights, or guardian. Grandparents and other relatives with whom the student resides and most foster parents are also considered "parents" under IDEA. A parent does not include the state if the state has guardianship over the child.

PBIS (Positive Behavioral Interventions and Supports)
PBIS is a general education, schoolwide approach utilized with students to create a positive student culture and individualized behavior supports to bring about a safe and effective learning environment.

Placement
The location, setting, services and supports in which the special education services and supports are delivered to the student that is specified in the child's IEP.

Present Levels of Academic Achievement and Functional Performance
A statement on the IEP that describes what the child knows and can do academically and non-academically, or functionally, at this time. (see Chapter 1)

PLAAF (Present Levels of Academic Achievement and Functional Performance), **PLEP** (Present Levels of Educational Performance) and **PLOP** (Present Levels of Performance)

All of these terms refer to The Present Levels of Academic Achievement and Functional Performance and are used interchangeably. They all refer to the data that describes the part of the IEP that identifies a student's strengths, challenges and needs that result from the child's disability. The Present Levels are the foundation for the development of the IEP goals, supports, and services.

PTI (Parent Training & Information Center)
The agency under the direction of the IDEA that is responsible for providing training and information to parents of children with disabilities living in areas served by the centers, particularly underserved parents and parents of children who may be inappropriately identified.

PWN (Prior Written Notice)

PWN is the written communication to the parent whenever the district proposes, or refuses to initiate, or change the identification, evaluation, educational placement, or provision of FAPE to a child.

Related Services

Related services means: "transportation and such developmental, corrective, and other supportive services as are required to assist a child with a disability to benefit from special education, and includes speech-language pathology and audiology services, interpreting services, psychological services, physical and occupational therapy, recreation, including therapeutic recreation, early identification and assessment of disabilities in children, counseling services, including rehabilitation counseling, orientation and mobility services, and medical services for diagnostic or evaluation purposes. Related services also include school health services and school nurse services, social work services in schools, and parent counseling and training." The following fourteen Related Services are detailed in 34 CFR Sec. 300.34 of Regulations:

Audiology Services

Audiology services are provided to students with hearing loss and/or auditory processing disorders to have adequate access to auditory information in their educational settings.

Counseling Services

Counseling services means services provided by qualified social workers, psychologists, guidance counselors, or other qualified personnel.

Medical Services

Medical services means services provided by a licensed physician to determine whether a child's medically related disability results in the child's need for special education and related services. *NOTE: medical services are only a related service under IDEA if they are for diagnostic or evaluative purposes.*

Occupational Therapy (OT)

OT means services provided by a qualified occupational therapist and includes improving, developing, or restoring functions impaired or lost through illness, injury, or deprivation; improving ability to perform tasks for independent functioning if functions are impaired or lost; and preventing, through early intervention, initial or further impairment or loss of function.

Orientation and Mobility Services

Orientation and mobility services means services provided to blind or visually impaired children by qualified personnel to enable those students to attain systematic orientation to and safe movement within their environments in school, home, and community; and includes teaching children the following, as appropriate: spatial and environmental concepts and use of information received by the senses (such as sound, temperature and vibrations) to establish, maintain, or regain orientation and line of travel (e.g., using sound at a traffic light to cross the street); to use the long cane or a service animal to supplement visual travel skills or as a tool for safely negotiating the environment for children with no available travel vision; to understand and use remaining vision and distance low vision aids; and other concepts, techniques, and tools.

Parent Counseling and Training

Parent counseling and training means assisting parents in understanding the special needs of their child; providing parents with information about child development; and helping parents to acquire the necessary skills that will allow them to support the implementation of their child's IEP.

Physical Therapy

Physical therapy means services provided by a qualified physical therapist. Psychological services includes administering psychological and educational tests, and other assessment procedures; interpreting assessment results; obtaining, integrating, and interpreting information about child behavior and conditions relating to learning; consulting with other staff members in planning school programs to meet the special educational needs of children as indicated by psychological tests, interviews, direct observation, and behavioral evaluations; planning and managing a program of psychological services, including psychological counseling for children and parents; and assisting in developing positive behavioral intervention strategies.

Recreation

Assessment of leisure function; therapeutic recreation services; recreation programs in schools and community agencies; and leisure education.

Rehabilitation Counseling Services

Rehabilitation counseling services means services provided by qualified personnel in individual or group sessions that focus specifically on career development, employment preparation, achieving independence, and integration in the workplace and community of a student with a disability. The term also includes vocational rehabilitation services provided to a student with a disability by vocational rehabilitation programs funded under the Rehabilitation Act of 1973.

School Health Services and School Nurse Services

School health services and school nurse services means health services that are designed to enable a child with a disability to receive FAPE as described in the child's IEP. School nurse services are services provided by a qualified school nurse. School health services are services that may be provided by either a qualified school nurse or other qualified person.

Social Work Services

Social work services in schools includes preparing a social or developmental history on a child with a disability; group and individual counseling with the child and family; working in partnership with parents and others on those problems in a child's living situation (home, school, and community) that affect the child's adjustment in school; mobilizing school and community resources to enable the child to learn as effectively as possible in his or her educational program; and assisting in developing positive behavioral intervention strategies.

(SLP) Speech-Language Pathology Services
Speech-language pathology services includes identification of children with speech or language impairments; diagnosis and appraisal of specific speech or language impairments; referral for medical or other professional attention necessary for the habilitation of speech or language impairments; provision of speech and language services for the habilitation or prevention of communicative impairments; and counseling and guidance of parents, children, and teachers regarding speech and language impairments.

Transportation
Transportation includes travel to and from school and between schools; travel in and around school buildings; and specialized equipment (such as special or adapted buses, lifts, and ramps), if required to provide special transportation for a child with a disability.

Referral
A written or verbal notice to a school district that a child may be in need of special education, is suspected of having a disability, and is in need of being evaluated in all suspected areas of disability. A referral sets specific timelines for the referral to special education process.

Resolution Session
An opportunity to resolve a dispute between a parent and a school district that must be offered to the parents after an Impartial Due Process Hearing was filed. See chapter on Procedural Safeguards.

RTI (Response to Intervention)
Response to Intervention (RTI) is a general education approach for struggling learners that provides multi-tiered support for learning and behavioral needs. Struggling learners are provided with interventions at increasing levels of intensity to accelerate their rate of learning. RTI cannot be used to delay or deny an evaluation for eligibility under the IDEA.

Screening
A screening is a brief standardized instrument or observation administered to a student to learn if they need more comprehensive testing in an educational area (OT, sensory, PT, etc.)

Special Education Services
The instructional support delivered by a school district's related service (see related services) providers, special education teachers and other support personnel to students who qualify for special education and have an IEP.

SY (School Year)
The number of instructional days and hours (typically 180 days) each year a district is in session for elementary, middle and secondary school students. Length of the school day varies by state.

SEA (State Educational Agency)
State educational agency or SEA means the state board of education or other agency or officer primarily responsible for the state supervision of public elementary schools and secondary schools, or, if there is no such officer or agency, an officer or agency designated by the Governor or by state law.

SMART Goals
IEP goals following five elements that create goals with a clearly understood objective. The acronym SMART stands for specific, measurable, achievable, relevant and time-bound, though there are several versions of this acronym.

SOP (Summary of Performance)
A Summary of Performance (SOP) is required for a child with
a disability whose eligibility under special education ends by
exceeding the age of eligibility or graduating with a regular
diploma. The local education agency must provide a summary
of academic achievement and functional performance, called the
SOP. The summary should make recommendations on how to
assist the student in meeting their postsecondary goals.

Transition Services
The term means "a coordinated set of activities for a child with a
disability that is designed to be within a results-oriented process,
that is focused on improving the academic and functional achievement of the child with a disability to facilitate the child's movement
from school to post-school activities, including post-secondary
education, vocational education, integrated employment (including
supported employment), continuing and adult education, adult services, independent living, or community participation; is based on
the individual child's needs, taking into account the child's strengths,
preferences, and interests; and (includes instruction, related services,
community experiences, the development of employment and other
post-school adult living objectives, and, when appropriate, acquisition of daily living skills and functional vocational evaluation."[24]

Transition Plan
The plan of action within the IEP that documents the specifics of
the transition services. (see Transition Services)

504 Plan
Section 504 of the Rehabilitation Act is a federal anti-
discrimination law which protects students from discrimination
based on disability. The 504 Plan is developed to ensure that a
child who has a disability receives accommodations that will
ensure their academic and functional success.

---

24 20 U.S.C. §1401(34)

RESOURCES

The best place to go when you are researching what the IDEA requires is right to the source: www.ed.gov. This is the website for the US Department of Education, and you can find the IDEA, its implementing Regulations, and many other helpful documents, guidance, and FAQ's.

Next best is your own state Department of Education . . . though we would be remiss if we didn't note that not all state Ed websites are helpful, and some of them are actually problematic or interpret the law in ways with which we disagree. Strongly. The USDE has a page where you can look up your own state or Territory's Department of Education: https://www2.ed.gov/about/contacts/state/index.html

An organization near and dear to our hearts for parents, attorneys, and advocates is COPAA, the Council of Parent Attorneys and Advocates, www.COPAA.org

We strongly recommend all things Wrightslaw for ongoing research and training . . . Pete and Pam Wright are friends and colleagues, and their work is always worth following: www.wrightslaw.com

APPENDIX A

A GUIDED SUMMARY OF RELEVANT PORTIONS OF THE FEDERAL SPECIAL EDUCATION LAW

The IDEA is codified at 20 USC 1400 et seq. That means 20 United States Code 1400 and the following chapters of the statute. It is the legal citation to the law. The special education regulations are found at 34 CFR 300. That is 34 Code of Federal Regulations 300, and following chapters of the regulations.

While we did not include the entirety of the IDEA in this Appendix because not all of it is relevant to our manual on IEPs, we did include summaries and links to five sections of the statute which are essential to be able to reference and understand the special education law. They are:

> What is the difference between a statute and a regulation? The easiest way to think of it is this: a statute is law that is passed by a legislative body. Here, the IDEA was passed by Congress. Regulations are meant to explain or augment the statute and are enacted by administrative agencies, here the United States Department of Education. So, Congress passed the IDEA and then the USDE passed the implementing regulations.

20 USC 1400: *Short Title, Findings, Purposes*

Why did we include this? This is where Congress summarizes why they passed the IDEA to begin with and puts the statute into context. There is some truly beautiful language to be found in this Section, and we feel that parents and educators should never lose sight of how far we have come from when students with disabilities literally had no legal right to attend public schools, let alone receive an appropriate education there. When you feel confused about why a rule exists or why there are certain mandates in the IDEA, going back to read this Section may enlighten you.

20 USC 1412: *State Eligibility*

This section defines FAPE (Free and Appropriate Public Education); "Child Find," which is the obligation that all school districts are required to identify, evaluate, and program for all students with disabilities who reside in their jurisdiction, regardless of whether they attend the public schools; LRE (Least Restrictive Environment), which is the cornerstone of ensuring that students with disabilities are allowed to attend the schools, classrooms, and activities that are offered to their nondisabled peers; and outlines many other obligations which local and state educational agencies must meet.

20 USC 1413: *Local Educational Agency Eligibility*

This one is a bit dry, and not one most parents or educators will need to "go to" frequently in their advocacy and professional efforts. However, it does have some very specific funding implications for state and local educational agencies, as well as some important language about the use of funds for early intervening services and charter schools.

20 USC 1414: *Evaluations, Eligibility Determinations, IEPs and Educational Placements*

This section is chock-full of information and is the focus of Chapters 1–8, since this is where we find the descriptions of the requirements for an IEP. In addition to that, Section 1414 covers the very complicated evaluation process in great detail, from initial evaluations to re-evaluations, and the standards for determining eligibility. It also outlines the requirements before determining that a student is no longer eligible for services. After defining IEPs, this section also defines the IEP Team and the members who are required to be part of the IEP Team, and more.

20 USC 1415: *Procedural Safeguards*

This is the section parents and students derive many of their legal protections from, and it is so important to understanding the IEP process that we devoted a separate chapter to summarizing the Procedural Safeguards. In addition to out-

> Don't forget to check your own local and state policies and laws to see if there are different or additional requirements for an IEP beyond what the federal law requires

lining the many ways in which parents are required to be included in the participation of their child's IEP and program, this section also outlines the various procedures which exist when parents and educators cannot agree on whether the student is eligible or whether the IEP is appropriate. It includes the law surrounding the right to Mediation and Due Process, as well as Complaint procedures.

20 USC 1400: WHY THE IDEA EXISTS

Note from Jen and Julie: This is the portion of the IDEA which explains why Congress enacted the Education for All Handicapped Children Act in 1975, later renamed the Individuals with Disabilities Education Act. It includes the staggering statistics of what life was like for children with disabilities in the United States prior to the legislation that protected them and establishes the purposes of the Act.

§1400. Short title; findings; purposes

20 USC 1412: WHAT STATES MUST DO

Note from Jen and Julie: The structure of the IDEA is that it offers funding to the States which agree to be bound by its terms. In other words, if the state wants the money (referred to as "assistance") associated with the IDEA, it must agree to comply with the mandates of the law. All States and US Territories have opted in, and therefore must follow the procedural and substantive requirements of the law. This Section of the IDEA explains the obligations that States must meet to be eligible for the funding, and includes the descriptions of FAPE (Free and Appropriate Public Education), and the other mandates of the statute. The IDEA has never been fully funded by Congress, leading many local and state educational agencies to bear significant additional costs in educating children with disabilities. We prefer to look at special education as an investment, not a cost. When done well, the burden on States will presumably be less down the road, when the child with a disability becomes an adult with skills.

Section 1412
§1412. State eligibility

20 USC 1413: WHAT LOCAL AND
CHARTER SCHOOLS MUST DO

Note from Jen and Julie: Just as Section 1412 discusses how state Educational Agencies can become eligible for the "assistance" (money) associated with complying with the IDEA, this section of the statute outlines how Local Educational Agencies become eligible. It also discusses eligibility and requirements for Charter Schools, among other things.

§1413. Local educational agency eligibility

20 USC 1414: EVALUATIONS, ELIGIBILITY, IEPS AND PLACEMENT

Note from Jen and Julie: While this book is an IEP Guide, designed to assist IEP Team Members in developing the IEP itself, prior to doing that, school districts are legally required to follow certain procedures in order to determine whether the student qualifies for an IEP to begin with. That starts with a referral to be evaluated for eligibility for special education. This Section of the IDEA explains that process, and the process for continued evaluation and considerations for eligibility beyond first identification. It also contains the eight federally mandated elements of an IEP that we break down in Part 2 of the manual.

§1414. Evaluations, eligibility determinations, individualized education programs, and educational placements

20 USC 1415: YOU CAN'T DO THAT
AND YOU MUST DO THIS

Note from Jen and Julie: For parents of students with disabilities, understanding your child's rights starts, but does not end, with understanding your Procedural Safeguards; these are the rules. For educators and related professionals, the procedures are also the "you can't do this" and the "you must do that" rules of the IDEA. They are so important (and lengthy, and complex) that we have an entirely separate chapter in the book to explain them. However, from time to time you should revisit the actual language of the statute, so here it is.

APPENDIX B

10 QUESTIONS YOU (PROBABLY) AREN'T ASKING AT YOUR CHILD'S IEP MEETING BUT SHOULD BE

1. "What standard do you use in this school to determine whether a child is on track academically, based on what data, and where does my child fall in this ranking?"

PRACTICAL TIP: When the team reports to you about how your child is performing on certain measures of progress in the curriculum, ask the team to define expected level for students without disabilities at this juncture in the school year/their education.

ASK FOR BENCHMARKS AND SCOPE AND SEQUENCE

2. "How are my child's social, behavioral, adaptive, and other functional skills? How do they impact him in school?"

PRACTICAL TIP: Ask for specific examples of these skills in both structured settings (like the classroom) and unstructured settings (like recess or lunch). Ask for specific examples for both academic and extra-curricular opportunities.

3. "Is there a proposed goal in this IEP for each identified area where his disability affects his involvement and progress in the general education curriculum?"

PRACTICAL TIP: Make sure to go through: academic, social, emotional, health, behavioral, and functional skills. If necessary, go through the Present Levels of Academic and Functional Performance portion of your child's IEP, and ask which goal addresses each area of impact."

4. "What data do you have to support the reported progress towards my child's goals? How did you measure them?"

PRACTICAL TIP: Research "SMART Goals" and make sure your IEP goals include these elements. If there is data that the team is claiming they collect, ask if you can be provided with that data.

5. "What services and supports will my child and the team working with her be provided in order for her to make progress on her goals and be involved in the general education curriculum?"

PRACTICAL TIP: Be sure to ask for details about BOTH the supports/modifications for your child AND for the team. This could include what training is required, consultations by other professionals to the educators, as well as the actual services and supports your child will be getting. Also, don't forget to ask about extra-curriculars and non-academics!

6. "How much of my child's day, including non-academic and extra-curricular activities, will he be spending with peers who do not have disabilities, and why?"

PRACTICAL TIP: Be sure to understand the Least Restrictive Environment provisions of the IDEA, which states that students with disabilities should be educated in the regular classroom to the maximum extent appropriate, and removal from that environment should only occur if supplementary aids and services cannot be provided to keep the child in mainstream.

7. "How will my child's participation in district and state-wide testing differ from her nondisabled peers, and why?"

PRACTICAL TIP: Be sure to ask how the proposed accommodations will be individualized, and whether your child really needs them in order to participate in the testing. Many times, a student's performance on district and statewide testing without accommodations is a good indicator of whether they are truly keeping up with their nondisabled peers academically.

8. "When, where, and how will my child's special education and related services be provided, and for how long?"

PRACTICAL TIP: This is where the "rubber meets the road" in terms of spelling out the exact hours of service and supports your child will be getting. Pay close attention to: location, frequency, service provider responsible, and start and end dates, including Extended School Year (ESY) services for students who may require them. Also, modifications are VERY IMPORTANT, and you want to know in particular if your child's curriculum AND/OR GRADES are being modified.

9. "How does this IEP address Transition to Adulthood, including appropriate measurable postsecondary goals, for my older student, and based on what assessments?"

PRACTICAL TIP: By a student's sixteenth birthday, his IEP must include services to address Transition to Adulthood, including postsecondary goals related to training, education, employment and, where appropriate, independent living skills. These services should be based on appropriate assessments done to address Transition. In some states, Transition must be planned even earlier than age sixteen. TRANSITION SERVICES ARE TO BE PROVIDED FOR ALL STUDENTS WITH IEPs, REGARDLESS OF CATEGORY OF DISABILITY.

10. "Where on my child's IEP are my concerns and input as the Parents noted?"

PRACTICAL TIP: The law requires IEP Teams to consider information provided by the Parents to the team, including Parent concerns for "enhancing the education" of their child. Your concerns and input should be documented in the IEP paperwork, as well as on Prior Written Notice/Written Prior Notice.

Watch this video from *Your Special Education Rights* on YouTube— Written Prior Notice: Actions Proposed/Refused

APPENDIX C

SCHOOL YEAR AND GRADE SUMMARY

Note from Jen and Julie: Because school years are different from calendar years, it can be confusing when you pick up an IEP and look at the date to remember what school year the student was in at that time. To make your life a little easier, we have come up with these forms which you can fill out for your students or children. We hope they keep you grounded in the child's educational history, and recommend keeping one of these taped to the inside of the folder you use for the child for ease of reference! We have filled out this one as an example, but feel free to copy the blanks for yourself.

STUDENT NAME: Jason Davis

SCHOOL YEAR	GRADE
2019–2020	Pre-K
2020–2021	Kindergarten
2021–2022	1st Grade
2022–2023	2nd Grade
2023–2024	3rd Grade
2024–2025	Repeat 3rd Grade
2025–2026	4th Grade

SCHOOL YEAR AND GRADE SUMMARY

STUDENT NAME: _____

SCHOOL YEAR   **GRADE**

_____   _____

_____   _____

_____   _____

_____   _____

_____   _____

_____   _____

_____   _____

_____   _____

_____   _____

_____   _____

_____   _____

_____   _____

_____   _____

ACKNOWLEDGMENTS

First and foremost, we want to thank Skyhorse Publishing for approaching us with the idea for this book. We loved working with them on our first book and greatly appreciate their confidence in us. In particular, Stephan Zguta was on this project from day one and we are indebted to him for his patience as we tried to comply with deadlines and respond to his emails while managing our absurdly busy professional and personal schedules. And a special thank you to Julia King, who was able to turn around the drawings for our chapters quickly and with great professionalism.

We want to acknowledge and thank the many educators we have talked to and heard from over the years who have shared with us their frustration and perspectives on special education law in general and the IEP process, in particular. We know being a teacher in today's world with so many competing demands placed on you is often a thankless job . . . so we are here to thank you!

For the families we represent and have represented, we are grateful to you for teaching us what is and isn't important to you when it comes to knowing your child's rights. We are far better able to explain the IEP process because we have had thousands of pre and post IEP meeting conversations with you where you have shared your experiences: the good, the bad, and the ugly. If it weren't for the parents of children with disabilities, we would not even have federal law to protect them.

Special thanks to our friend and colleague, Attorney Melissa Gagne, for writing the foreword to the book. Since she has occupied every seat at the IEP table (teacher, parent, administrator, and attorney for children), her insight and support mean a great deal to us.

We are constantly working to improve the "system" through our involvement in two key organizations at the state and national level. Thank you to SEEK (Special Education Equity for Kids of Connecticut) and COPAA (Council of Parent Attorneys and Advocates). Our colleagues in these organizations include some of the true heroes and pioneers in the field of special education advocacy and disability civil rights, and we are exceedingly proud to learn from you every day.

Julie wishes to thank her husband, Steve, and her children, Nick and Alex, for their support and patience with her long hours in the office while she advocates for families throughout Connecticut and many other states. She also thanks all of the families she works with on behalf of their children with disabilities. As Julie's mother used to say, her job provides her with lots of emotional currency. Writing this book also provides her hope that as many parents as possible are better informed about the IEP process, thus giving them a leg up on improving their child's success.

Jen thanks her incredibly supportive family: Chad Gleason, James Swan, and Marisa Swan, all of her extended family and offspring, especially the late Bill Laviano who brought Jen and Julie together all those years ago. There is no way she could do a fraction of what she is able to accomplish without your patience and the many sacrifices you have made along the way. Huge gratitude to the entire team at Laviano & Gagne, who keep her on her toes and laughing along the way. Tremendous appreciation also goes to her clients, who have been patient in sharing her time while she finished this book during IEP Season!

We are both fortunate to have some of the best friends in the world, many of whom are teachers, advocates, and lawyers themselves. We appreciate you listening to us vent about this field and for caring about the children we serve. You show up at our events, spread the word about our projects, and generally make us able to do our jobs without quitting and opening up a flower shop! Thank you!

Finally, to all individuals with disabilities, whether school age or beyond: We have learned more from you than we have from any statute, book, or manual. Thank you most of all.

—Jen and Julie